Copyright © 2016 by Justine Atkinson

All rights reserved. No part of this book may be used or reproduced in any manner whatsoever without written permission except in the case of brief quotations embodied in critical articles and reviews.

Cartmel Characters

Modern Life in a Medieval Village

Written and photographed by
Justine Atkinson

Designed by Jamie Young

Edited by CopyCats

Contents

Introduction 9

David Unsworth
A man of his generation 12

Simon Rogan
A chef in touch with his surroundings 20

Tony Biggins
A.K.A. Boris the biker and the builder 26

Rachelle Bell
The eco-fashionista from Cartmel 34

Sweeney Bobs of Cartmel
A day in the life of the local barber 42

Billy and Mick Shaw
One dog and his man 44

Jean and Howard Johns
Founders of the pudding that conquered the world 50

Reverend Nick Devenish and the Priory Church
A significant place of welcome 58

Jimmy Moffatt
The village horse whisperer 66

Jonathan Garratt
Racecourse director and pony enthusiast 74

John Kerr
Cartmel's rare-book dealer 82

Lydia Crowe
The elegant lady in the baggy coat 90

Richard English
The Yorkshire lad with Cumbrian charm 96

Steve Chamberlain
Chief proprietor of Chamberlains' Gift Emporium 104

Dr Richard Fell
The man with a thousand and one stories 106

Tiffany Hunt
The lady with a legacy 114

Lord Hugh Cavendish
The green-fingered Lord 122

Beth Conroy
The diary of a party girl 132

Linda and David Crabtree
A couple at the heart of the community 140

Rachel Battersby
The devoted Headteacher 148

Dr Paul Williams
Headteacher at Cartmel Priory School 156

George Broadhurst
The man who's seen it all 158

Introduction

A primal heart still beats in the unchanged village of Cartmel, nestled in the county of Cumbria, one of England's most beautiful areas of outstanding natural beauty. Time seems to have stood still in this medieval settlement with its historic buildings and landscapes, which have survived attacks from Henry VIII and Oliver Cromwell's troops, with the bullet holes still there to prove it. Today, while the rest of the world is swallowed up by chain stores and globalisation, Cartmel has retained its individuality and continues to live according to its own script. Its old-world charm is evident in the Priory Church (built by William Marshal in the 12th century), a wooden notice board from the late 1800s that still hangs on the wall by the Gatehouse, and the chimes from one of Britain's oldest clocks that can still be heard across the village every hour.

Cartmel is famous for its fine dining; the village boasts a two Michelin-starred restaurant, and a world-conquering sticky toffee pudding. At various times throughout the year the population triples in size as just over 15,000 people pour into the village for the annual return of Cartmel Races. As the fair arrives, horse carts and numerous vendors trek bravely across the small and narrow stone bridge as they make their way to the racecourse.

The village has always played a significant role in my life. I was brought up a mile away and some of my earliest memories are of my grandfather coming to pick me up from outside my door on his horse-drawn carriage. I could have been no older than five years old but I remember the black Shire horses dwarfing me, and their covered eyes and leather muzzles daunting me as they thrust their heads from side to side breathing heavily. From there we would ride together down the narrow lanes from my house to Cartmel Show, where he would parade his horses and I would sample the local fudge with my grandmother. These early memories of Cartmel being a hub of festivity are etched into my memory and as I grew up we started to attend the Races. My Mum and I would play on the waltzers until our heads spun. As I got older my Mum was replaced with my friends, and we would spend the whole day at the racecourse in the summer hanging out and playing on the rides.

At secondary school we did cross-country running through the park and paddled in the beck. These were some of the luxuries of growing up in a place surrounded by nature. Our childhoods were full of freedom - we built dens, walked in the woods, took off on our bikes to find adventures, and felt safe and protected, surrounded by a community who knew who we were and looked out for us. This shaped me into the person I am today, someone who values community, nature and adventure.

But it was only when I returned from university that I fully integrated into the Cartmel village community. In between graduating and trying to find my life path I undertook various types of part-time work in Cartmel and the surrounding area. For seven months I worked in the saucing department of Cartmel Sticky Toffee Pudding. Every morning I drove to 'Pudding World' (as I nicknamed it), put on my white overalls and hand-ladled thousands and thousands of puddings.

Some of my fondest memories of Cartmel come from working in the Royal Oak pub, under different landlords to the ones who run it now. It was here that I worked for an infamous landlord who told me that I was in the 'University of Life' and I would learn more there than at any higher education establishment, and in a way he was right. We grew into a type of dysfunctional family who would bicker, misbehave and make up all in the same hour. We ate, drank, and did whatever we pleased, most of us were always late, and the majority of us were sacked at least once. But together our unique characters combined to bring the pub to life and provided a central hub for the locals of the village. I think it was in this space of honesty and camaraderie that I learnt more about myself than anywhere else. In an evening I could go from serving former surgeons of the Royal family, to scientists and famous jockeys, to builders and those who have lived in the village all their lives. Each one came in for their evening pint, and despite their differences they were united by time and place and would spend the evening exchanging stories. I witnessed fights spilling out into the Square, and an old man with narcolepsy bringing in his accordion to provide an impromptu performance that entertained the whole pub until he fell asleep on the bar. Moments like these stay with you, and it was when working in the Royal Oak that I first conceived the idea to document the characters in the village.

This book draws on these experiences and the close relationships I have developed with most of the characters featured here. Each chapter starts with an anecdote taken from the person's life and then uses this to explore their story. It reveals the array of personalities who bring Cartmel to life. Comprised of interviews with young and old generations this book will provide you with a revealing account of what lies behind this quintessentially British village.

David Unsworth

-

A man of his generation

Summer was approaching and a warm breeze swept through the racecourse, carrying with it the last sweet aromas of spring. Suddenly the peace and quiet was rudely broken by the clattering spurts of metal and a burst of smoke when a rider turned the key and kick-started his black motorbike. As the bike began to chunter out of the racecourse gates the rider looked to his right and braked, placing his feet on the ground for balance. 'Fill me up please, Ernest' he shouted to a little man sat at the gates. Ernest Unsworth was in his usual spot, sat on a small stool under a tree, surrounded by cans of petrol waiting for fuel-thirsty clients to get their fill. Today had been a good day, and with only a few cans left he decided to shut up shop and go for a pint. The year was 1921 and motorbikes and cars were starting to become more accessible after Henry Ford democratised car prices through mass production. Ernest finished up and headed over to the Royal Oak pub for his well-earned pint of ale.

Inside the pub he stood at the side of the bar supping his freshly poured beer. The bar owner returned from the till to give him his change, and in a thick northern accent Ernest loudly declared 'you know the years of the horse and cart are numbered now, give it twenty or thirty years and we'll all be driving motorcars!' The bar owner and punters nodded politely but they did not share his vision, to them the end of the horse and cart seemed like a distant future that may never come. But Ernest was ahead of his time, an innovative entrepreneur who could see a bright future for the motorcar, and he wanted to capitalise on it in his hometown of Cartmel.

By 1922 he had sold enough cans of petrol to rustle up the £400

David Unsworth

he needed to buy the plot of land upon which he would realise his dream. His land ran from the barber's shop right down to the little river, and he worked with his family to transform it into the first modern-day garage in Cartmel. Although it took a couple of years to establish itself, by 1930 his vision was achieved. The age of transport was in full swing and his bustling corner offered garage services and a petrol station to the locals. This garage became known as 'Unsworth's Yard' and was a true family-run business. Ernest ran the garage, while his son Percy drove the wagons and handled the mechanics, and his three daughters worked to serve petrol, drive taxis and handle the administration of the company. For almost three generations the garage provided employment for Ernest's whole family.

Following in the footsteps of his forefathers

David Unsworth (the grandson of Ernest) is an affable and articulate character. His dual persona combines a down-to-earth Northern lad who enjoys playing football and a good beer, with a food and drink connoisseur who has a strong aptitude for business. David is one of the few remaining villagers who was born and raised in Cartmel, and when we sit chatting I can see how deeply rooted he is here as he tells me stories from his family's 150-year history in the village.

David's family first moved to Cartmel in 1866. At the time his great-grandfather was landed gentry and lived in a large house on Aynsome Road, surrounded by vast acres of land equipped with its own stables and servants' quarters. They were living the high life, invited to posh social events, eating fine foods and being waited on hand and foot. Unfortunately though, this lifestyle was short-lived: since his great grandfather died very young they lost all their wealth, forcing them to dramatically downsize. They moved into the village Square where his great-grandmother, faced with lots of hungry mouths to feed, had to start working for a living. It was unusual for women to work at that time, and you can be sure the village gossips revelled in discussing the situation the Unsworth family were faced with. But ignoring this gossip, great-grandmother Unsworth used her last remaining savings to set up a sweet shop in the corner house on the Square, which she ran successfully for many years.

This act of entrepreneurship set in motion generations of innovation and pioneering ideas, which firmly rooted the Unsworth family as an important fixture in Cartmel. As we know, the next generation - David's grandfather Ernest - created the first petrol station and garage in Cartmel. This was passed down the generations and was first taken over by David's father, then later handed to David and his brother. It ran until 2000 when it was no longer viable to own a small independent petrol station or garage, as multinational companies outsized local businesses. However, the remarkable forward-thinking and ingenuity of Ernest Unsworth provided a foundation for his family for many years to come.

Realising the changing market, in 1998 David and his brother Peter took their first step in transforming Unsworth's Yard. They closed down the petrol station and built the Mallard Tea Shop. Well-situated, the Mallard still runs as a successful quaint teashop managed by David's sister, Alison, catering for walkers and the considerable market of retired people in the village. Seeing the success of this café, and the continued demise of garage work, David and his brother decided to take the Yard in an entirely new direction.

The transformation of Unsworth's Yard

Combining their knowledge of, and love for, food and beverages, in 2010 David and Peter Unsworth lay the foundation stone paving the way for a new era in Unsworth's Yard. By 2011 they had rebranded and reopened a new complex of artisan food businesses, tucked away in the shadow of the Priory Church. Today, David Unsworth and his family have transformed a struggling garage into a vibrant food complex. Their vision was to create a foodie's paradise in Cartmel, somewhere that could provide organic products, each handpicked from a sustainable producer. David has stated that 'it's important to us that people understand where their food and drink comes from, so nothing comes into the yard without us knowing 100% where it comes from, who made it, and why it's been made'.

The yard is filled with many well-sourced food delights. As you enter, you are met by the warm, yeasty smell of baked bread, freshly kneaded and baked in The Bread Shed that morning. To accompany this, Cartmel Cheeses offers an eclectic range of cheeses from either St James Dairy Farm or organic producers right across Europe. David's personal favourite is his wine shop that abides by the same ethos, and each product is carefully sourced to ensure that he knows the story behind the people making it. David also expanded outside his Yard and created a food market that takes place in Cartmel on the first Friday of every month. It provides space for local artisan producers to showcase their products, including chocolatiers, Mediterranean delicacies, local butchers, cake makers, chutney makers, and an Indian spice merchant. In an age where local artisan shops are diminishing with the increasing dominance of chain stores, and when the origin of most of the food we consume is unknown, Unsworth's Yard is offering a space where artisan producers both local and global are able to thrive.

Together the brothers have also worked to create a microbrewery inside the Yard, spearheaded by David's brother Peter three years ago. It took Peter three months to learn the art of brewing ale, and he decided to purchase equipment that would enable him to create their own custom-made Cartmel brews on site. This isn't the first time a brewery has been built in Cartmel: in the medieval and Victorian periods the local pubs created their beer in-house

Peter Unsworth in his brewery

before large breweries took over the market. Even more recently, in 1998, Nick Murray, the then-owner of the Cavendish Arms in Cartmel, attempted to create his own brewery, but he was ahead of his time and it never really took off. Now there are around 38 different microbreweries in Cumbria, and more and more discerning drinkers are turning their attention to locally brewed ales, so the market was just right for the creation of the Cartmel Ale.

The Unsworths have now developed four carefully brewed craft ales in Unsworth's Yard Brewery, each name inspired by a chapter of history from the village. 'Cartmel Pennisula' was their debut ale, it recognizes the historical location of the Cartmel Peninsula in Lancashire by placing the Lancashire rose on the front of the bottle. Their second beer, 'Last Wolf', pays homage to the wolf killed at Humphrey Head by Sir Edgar Harrington's men. Sir Edgar promised half his lands and his daughter Adela's hands to whichever Knight could kill the wolf. Their 'Sir William Marshal's Crusader Gold' beer is a tribute to Sir William Marshal, founder of the Priory Church and witness to the signing of the Magna Carta. Finally, there is the 'Cartmel's Famous Festival' ale. This is named after the many festivals hosted in the Cartmel Peninsula since the Middle Ages, when the Priory's monks held annual horse races. Modern racing, shows and cultural events keep this spirit alive, and this pale ale is a reminder of festival days both past and still to come.

The brewing takes place in the Yard, and is set behind a glass wall so that punters can watch Peter in action, and sample brews from the tap before they buy. The beer is sold in the local pubs in the village including the Royal Oak and the Priory Hotel, and also farther afield in neighbouring villages. Each week the Unsworth's Yard Brewery produces and sells 2,500 pints, so there is a great future ahead for this local enterprise.

In the heart of the community

With family and community at the heart of everything they do, Unsworth's Yard is the epitome of Cartmel Village spirit. It is a unique business that has provided work for almost three generations, first as a garage, and now as a fine selection of artisan food shops. Although the site has transformed dramatically over the last few years, it still continues to provide employment for the whole Unsworth family: as I mentioned, David's sister, Alison, runs the Mallard Tea Shop. Their younger sister works for her, his brother Peter runs the brewery, and he runs the wine shop. 'This is one of our biggest achievements', David says enthusiastically, 'many businesses pass from generation to generation from the same site, but for it to still be carrying the family in a completely different industry is pretty unique'.

The Unsworths have been at the heart of the community in Cartmel for over a century. In that time they have witnessed the transformation of the village from a small, innocuous place to a hub of entrepreneurs with new visions and ideas. Cartmel has a special place in David's heart and in his opinion it will never be famous for just one thing. 'With all the things on offer, Cartmel Sticky Toffee Pudding, the Priory, or Unsworth's Yard it's the sum of the parts that makes it unique', David says. 'People come to Cartmel for different reasons, the people who come to look around the Priory are very different to the type of people who come to the racecourse to drink and bet. There is something for everyone'. This is the reason why Cartmel has evolved to be such a special and well-loved place, it is brimming with things to offer. The Unsworths have been contributing to this for decades, constantly reinventing themselves, and doing it with a vision of benefiting those around them, both their family and their community.

Simon Rogan

-

A chef in touch with his surroundings

Deep in the heart of Cartmel Fell lies an area of 20 miles of forest, marshland, fields and bushes. At first glance it seems deserted and eerily still, with only a whisper of wind brushing through the fog as it falls into the fell. But then something stirs in the bushes, like the sound of a small animal rustling in search of food. But this is no animal, it's the chief forager of L'Enclume restaurant in Cartmel. He makes his way out of the bushes, through brambles and bracken, plucking his clothes on sharp thorns on his way. It's early September and the hedgerows are lined with the sweet berries of autumn, blanketing the dry-stonewalls. One-by-one he collects the berries, placing them in his basket, keeping his eyes open for the next find. He spots a velvety fan of deep autumnal-brown mushrooms flocked together amongst the leaves like upside-down ladies from the 19th century, their large skirts on show. Kneeling down, he collects them until his bags are filled.

The fells of Cartmel are lined with deceptive plants, ones that look harmless but may be hallucinogenic, secrete poison, or burn your skin. The forager treads carefully, using his vast knowledge to identify and pick foraged goods. In amongst the dangerous plants the fells are lined with all manner of treats: wild fungi, garlic, plants and flowers. These include the herb sweet cicely, which is local to the area, and of which you can eat any part of the plant, from the light green leaves to the white flowers and pointed seeds that smell of aniseed when crushed.

There is something primeval about foraging, an instinctual part of our psyche that reconnects us to the land. However, our desire for, and knowledge of, foraging has almost entirely diminished since the increasing

Simon Rogan ©Simon Rogan

reliance on supermarkets dictates what is on our plate. It now takes extensive learning to be able to take us back to basics.

What these fields unveil is the mystical story of food, embroidered with folklore and ancient cultures. Simon Rogan has used this to his advantage. He says: 'The hills of Cumbria hold one of nature's best nature larders,' and these plentiful delicacies are used to showcase the tastes, textures and fragrances of the surrounding natural world. Simon Rogan has used wild and wonderful foraged foods, alongside organic produce grown on his farm to help make L'Enclume one of the best restaurants in the world.

Simon in Cartmel

I can remember when Simon first arrived in Cartmel, the chatter amongst the villagers of a new chef coming to take over the Old Forge house and transform it into a new restaurant. No one knew what to expect, and I don't think anyone could have predicted the resounding success he has transformed it into, and the impact this would have on the village. Simon was first introduced to Cartmel following a call from a friend who worked as a recruitment consultant, who suggested he go to take a look at some premises in the village. Upon seeing the space, he could see his dream of becoming a top chef unfolding there. So in 2002 he took a risk and packed up his life in Littlehampton and moved with his wife Penny Tapsell to this remote, medieval village in Cumbria.

Prior to arriving in the village Simon had admired the work of French chef Marc Veyrat who is famous for his use of alpine herbs and flowers, creating new and innovative methods to incorporate them into his dishes. Inspired by this use of natural ingredients and a variety of other influences, serendipity had brought him and Cartmel together. Business was tough at first, and L'Enclume was only open for half the week. But as Simon began to experiment with the rich environment around him, his business really took root, and in 2005 the restaurant picked up its first Michelin star. Since then Simon has created an empire in the village and beyond. He has his own 12-acre farm in Cartmel valley that now supplies L'Enclume and many of Simon's other restaurants across the country, enhancing the connection between nature and the plate. His particular methods of blending organic ingredients and flavours make each dish on the menu as intriguing as the one before, which makes dining at L'Enclume a truly unique experience.

Next to his farm, Simon later also opened Rogan's together with his wife Penny. This restaurant sits around the corner just over the stone bridge and was a welcome addition to the village. I would spend many an evening there drinking wine and eating cheese during the summer break from university. Since then, this has also become another fine-dining restaurant to add to his empire in Cartmel.

Since 2002, when I first heard of the founding of L'Enclume, Simon has been the catalyst of change in the village. He received another Michelin star in 2012, and from this L'Enclume and with it the village reached new levels of fame. Cartmel was listed in the *New York Times* 2014 top 52 places to visit in the world, listing L'Enclume as the main attraction. It was a surprise to the villagers to see their home at number 44, alongside other entries such as Cape Town, Namibia, Athens and the Arctic Circle. We seemed rather small in comparison. But this was just the start, and other rave reviews followed from the *Telegraph*, *Guardian*, *Daily Mail*, and mentions on Chris Evans' Radio 2 show who described Cartmel as a 'thimble full of diamonds' following his visit. Tourism in the village has significantly increased, and at peak time you will see someone on every corner snapping pictures of what was once a sleepy medieval village. These are just some of the things Simon has brought to Cartmel.

Early starts

Simon has always had an interest in cooking. His parents both worked long hours so from a young age he was left to prepare the evening meal. Through this he taught himself how to cook basic meals, and at 13 he got a weekend job at a Greek restaurant. After leaving school he increased his hours and worked four days with them, and started catering college one day a week. After only a few weeks he decided that this wasn't for him and he went to work in a posh hotel to learn from the best - after all he had his eyes set on becoming a top chef.

The restaurant industry is probably one of the toughest industries, and working in a professional kitchen is an intense and high-stress job, so you have to learn quickly or you will fall behind. Luckily for Simon, his talents flourished in this environment. He was trained by some of the leading experts in the country, including Marco Pierre White and Jean-Christophe Novelli. He also made appearances on MasterChef and the Great British Menu, putting himself at the forefront of culinary expertise.

Stubborn and independent-minded, Simon didn't want to work for other people, but instead wanted to build his own empire. His drive motivated him to creatively use the skills he learnt from working under a vast array of chefs, thus forging his own direction. Now he has achieved what he set out to do; he took over from Gordon Ramsey at the highly acclaimed Claridge's restaurant in London, now called Fera at Claridge's, taken from the Latin word for 'wild'. Here he has put his own stamp on the food, and built on the approach he took at L'Enclume to create 'an à la carte menu with a creative and natural take on modern British cuisine' (Fera at Claridge's website, 2016). He also runs The French and Mr Coopers, bringing a new chapter of natural produce to Manchester. In addition, he offers exclusive dining experiences in L'Enclume and Fera at Claridge's, where six people sample a surprise menu of ingredients taken from his farm, which are cooked and explained right in front of them. This busy schedule of projects means that Simon has to juggle his time between all the restaurants, moving between Cartmel, Manchester and London, ensuring they are well-managed and his dishes are executed with excellence. This means a lot of early starts.

Simon and the Cartmel community

Simon, L'Enclume and his farm are very much integrated into the community in Cartmel and the surrounding area. The local school children go to the farm to help to plant and grow the produce that is used to prepare the dishes in his restaurants. He also works with Cumbria Tourism, inviting young people to spend time on his farm and in his kitchen. He employs local workers to transform his buildings, creating jobs and enterprise in the village. He is the reason that Cartmel is the success story it is today, and why every small artisan business in Cartmel is thriving. He has used his work to complement people's experience of the village, reconnecting them with the earth and environment. This can only be a winning combination.

Tony Biggins

–

A.K.A. Boris the biker and the builder

'I was brought up in a caravan just at the top field in between Allithwaite and Cartmel,' Boris says as he looks down into his cup of tea. 'I was born in Cartmel, in Bankside Farm up Holker Bank, my granddad was a tenant farmer there, and my dad worked on the farm. Granddad retired and all of a sudden my family became homeless, so me, my two sisters and Mum and Dad had to live in a caravan. At the time we didn't know anything different, but it was a tin house. It was hard for my mum, but we got through it, and after four years we moved into a council house. Then at 17 we moved to this house at Headless Cross, I bought it and I've been here since'.

This was quite an introduction to someone who has lived in Cartmel his whole life, which is what makes Boris' story an unusual one. Boris grew up in Cartmel in the 1970s and 80s and after quite a shocking start, as we talk, his experience during his formative years in the village begins to unfold.

Pulling a plastic trolley stacked with rolled newspapers, a young boy makes his way out of the paper shop. He shouts a brisk goodbye to the owner, Mrs Robinson, who peers around the till as he wheels out, ensuring nothing is lost on her watch. He knows the route, and methodically pulls piles of newspapers along cobbles and up pebble paths, neatly posting one through every door on his list. Needing no map, he knows the face behind every door, and greets each one he meets with the appropriate level of enthusiasm. At the end of his loop he returns the empty trolley back to the shop in exchange for his 50

Boris (Tony Biggins)

pence payment and a bottle of pop.

As the years went by, the same young boy turned into a rebellious teen, too adventurous to settle down and attend school. He and his other tearaway friends spent their days terrorising the neighbourhood riding their motorbikes in the park, trying to leave as many tire tracks in their wake as possible. The loud roars of the exhausts could be heard across the village, and as the local residents' anger grew someone had to take control. One dark night a raucous group of young boys set off on the two-mile journey from Cartmel to Allithwaite to attend the Friday night dance. Bottles of beer in hands they laughed and roared together, each trying to outshine the other in a young-macho show of bravado. Intimidated, residents peeped through their curtains and shook their heads at the youths. As they walked past the school a car slowed down to a halt and rolled down its window. For a moment they expected to be disciplined by a disapproving elderly resident from the village for being in the way, but as the face appeared through the darkness they saw it is was local policeman, Ted Harrington, one of the only people the group would listen to. 'Get in you lot!' he shouted, reaching over to open the door. Glad to be spared the walk the four lads got in and he drove them up to the dance. 'I'll be back to get you later' he shouted back as they got out, drawn like moths to the beckoning call of the disco lights. He later returned to pick the lads up from the dance, to prevent them from causing trouble on their way back.

A good guy, Ted Harrington combined an authoritative personality with humble public service. He tried his best to contain the youths, still ensuring they had their freedom, knowing that trying to restrain them would only cause more problems. In his efforts to do this he even bargained with the local council, and got the boys a plot of land at the back of Cartmel Park far away from houses. This appeased both the residents, keeping down the noise pollution and kept the young lads happy. 'There were only two rules,' Boris recalls, 'we had to wear helmets and make a little buggy to take the bikes up to the park, as we weren't allowed to ride them there. We thought that this was a reasonable compromise so we stuck to it.'

For Boris, this was a different time in the village, there was a family behind every door, most of whom had been there for generations. He felt part of a real community, he knew everyone and felt like this was a place where he belonged. As time went on this sense of place and belonging slowly waned.

The history of the Borises

Tony Biggins has been nicknamed Boris since his early days in the schoolyard. His dad was also given this nickname, and so was his dad before him. They were all born in Cartmel, and his dad and granddad worked as farmers all of their lives. His mother came to Cartmel from Sunderland after she was evacuated along with her brother during World War II. In a romantic tale of love between two sets of siblings, his mum and dad married, and his mum's brother and his dad's sister also married. In the end they all settled in Cartmel and raised both their families close to each other.

    As we talk Boris explains that both his dad and uncle fought during World War II. At that time there was a lot of pressure on young men to become a soldier, and even though they could have been exempted, pressure mounted and both decided to join up. The scars of war remained with them all their lives. His uncle fought as a Royal Air Force bomber, and was shot down in Belgium. He was presumed dead, but was rescued and went on an undercover journey through cellars, under horse carts through Holland and back to the UK. Six months later he arrived back and knocked on his door, greeted by his mum who fainted in shock as she opened the door.

Unable to speak about their trauma, Boris first heard this story at his uncle's funeral decades later. His father also served in Belgium for three years, but never discussed his experience. The only time he hinted at memories was when an American war movie came on the TV and he immediately ordered them to turn it off. A generation of young men forced into war came back different people, scarred with the memories of their experiences. His father and uncle came back and returned to their families, his dad went back to farming, and carried on like nothing had happened. Like many returned soldiers he became emotionally closed, and this had a huge impact on the type of relationship he had with Boris.

Boris the IIIrd - the biker and the builder

The only career advice Boris's dad ever gave him was not to be a farmer, and after his childhood experiences he listened to him. Boris left school and went to train as a builder. He is a self-made man and has relied on his charisma and ingenuity to guide him through life. He has worked in many different places during that time, some local and some international. In 1992 he was contracted for seven months to work in the Falkland Islands airport. 'This was one of my most challenging and memorable jobs, as it was cold, wet and a long way from home,' he recalls. The only rays of light were the characters he met there, people from all over the world who put their cultural differences aside and formed friendships. 'There was this one Welsh guy who looked just like Clint Eastwood, tall with a chiselled jawline. But no one messed with him, he was a dangerous man, a black belt in karate and carried a pistol everywhere with him', Boris explains, chuckling, as he casts his memory back.

He came back to work for the building division in the Council for many years before starting his own local freelance building company with another local guy, John Burton. Together they make an invincible team, and work all across the local area. However, over the last few years, work in Cartmel has reduced considerably. Boris puts this down to one reason: 'It's the number of holiday homes that have been bought in the village, the people who live in those houses don't use local builders, but bring in outside labour forces to do the work. It all chips away at the business for locals'.

As well as being a full-time builder, in his spare time Boris is also an avid biker. After spending his youth biking with his mates on Cartmel Park, he developed a passion for motorbikes. He now buys old, run-down bikes and does them up. As with everything he does, this was self-taught, influenced by his dad and uncle who were also interested in bikes. He has five MV Agustas in his garage, all bought as scrap and carefully restored. Every summer Boris takes one out for a spin across Europe, as he and a group of his friends take to the road, with no plans, hotel bookings or other reservations, just for the thrill of adventure.

As we sit in his living room I see a miniature bike small enough for a toddler to ride, which he rides occasionally at off-road races. There is also an eclectic array of animals and objects including a parrot named Captain Jack, who squawks in a large cage to the side of the sofa, and some (many) Pendelfin rabbit ornaments belonging to his partner Jude, all neatly positioned in a large wooden cabinet in the corner of the room. A small French bulldog, nicknamed Bat-Pig jumps up at me as I sip my Vimto, and out of the window stands a life-size plastic donkey with a for-sale sign on the front lawn. This is quite a mix for only a small living room, but I think this is reflective of Boris's personality. He is a 'jack of all trades', a builder, bike fanatic, devoted partner and musician, and he has developed a life for himself in Cartmel to mirror this.

Boris in Cartmel

Boris has spent his whole life in Cartmel. During that time he has seen it change from a community he was part of, to one in which he felt more and more like an outsider. He plays in a band called Rusty Bullets, who perform all across the area including once a month in Cartmel. The band attracts a large crowd, and through each performance he feels his place in Cartmel is momentarily reaffirmed.

But for him the pubs in Cartmel have changed dramatically from having a strong local drinking culture, to becoming more food and tourist orientated. Each night Boris used to go down to one of the local pubs, and without any planning was guaranteed to bump into a village character or two. But now that has disappeared. For him Cartmel has changed from being full of working-class families and a real sense of community, to a pretentious place full of holiday homes and middle-class homeowners. The class differences become apparent as he explains that according to local gossip 'there was a meeting in the village which discussed the possibility of taking the part of Cartmel I live in, Headless Cross, out of Cartmel, and call it the lower hamlet of Allithwaite so that it doesn't "lower the tone" of the village. This is what we're up against!' he says despairingly. Although the changes in the village have been extremely beneficial for others, for Boris it has meant being excluded from a place his family have called home for generations. For now he intends on staying in the village as it still has a special place in his heart, but he is uncertain about the future.

A cloud of that potent musty aroma of second hand clothes hits the nostrils, as the glass door swings open and two young ladies make their way inside. Dressed in vintage inspired outfits and handbags at the ready, they embark on their mission of the day - to find that charity shop steal. The rails are lined with an array of oversized, garishly coloured items spanning the last three decades, and the hunt is on to spot the best pieces to accompany their eccentric tastes. They part ways, each taking a different side of the shop, and the race begins. Each one shuffles through the racks and rummages through mountains of clothes, flicking past old skirts, shirts and tops pulling out the best picks. Arms filled with a variety of different colours, prints and styles, they hit the changing rooms to sort through their finds.

Like a scene from what would be a low-budget version of *Pretty Woman* they pop out in turn to show the other their favourite outfits, ensuring that they are in keeping with their vintage and alternative inspired fashion. In the end they decide on a variety of items including two eighties-style Nightingales print T-shirts with thick ribbed cotton, both at the bargain price of £2 each; a pair of monochrome hippy print trousers by George for £1.50; a vintage Laura Ashley dress for £2; a Vivienne Westwood T-shirt for £1.50; and River Island printed trousers for £3 - which were still retailing for £40 on the River Island website. Happy, they make their way to the till to bag their second hand swag!

There is a new generation of twenty-somethings who have left behind the consumerist values of the nineties. The days of ladies aspiring for lives out of *Sex in the City* are fading, and now there is a whole wave of young,

Rachelle in her caravan

fashionable women who value independent styles rather than coveting the latest Prada or Gucci bag. The economic crunch, and increasing awareness of the environment might have had a lot to do with this shift, but more and more ladies are creating their own image, rather than trying to look like something out of the latest fashion magazine. With tight-fitting jeans, old-school trainers, flamboyant patterns, they are effortlessly and affordably creating the urban bohemian look of an eco-fashionista.

Rachelle Bell, the eco-fashionista from Cartmel

According to the *Urban Dictionary* an eco-fashionista is someone 'in their 20s, who values independent thinking, counter culture and progressive politics [...] who rejects the culturally ignorant attitudes of mainstream consumers, and is often seen wearing vintage and environmentally sustainable clothing or fashions'. A regular second hand shopper, vintage lover, environmental activist and fashion writer, at 26 years old Rachelle encapsulates all these qualities.

Rachelle grew up in Cartmel spending her formative years in the safety of the close-knit community. She would spend the days playing outdoors with her friends, with only one rule – be home before dark. It was the days before technology really transformed everything and she would use the Priory Clock as her watch, obediently going home on time each evening. Every month she would save her pocket money and spend it on English Lakes ice creams, and occasionally the latest Beanie Baby from The Larch Tree. It's a happy place to grow up with a childhood filled with inquisitive outdoor adventure and play. 'When I started university I would joke with my new friends who were brought up in the city, that I was a feral child who spent most of her time in the woods building dens and playing on her friends' farms', Rachelle jokes. A country girl at heart, she moved to Preston to undertake a degree in Fashion Styling and Promotion, which enhanced her creative abilities and developed her skills in marketing, creative writing and fashion campaigns.

Her passion for discovering bargains started when she was at university. She wanted an affordable and unique style on a student budget, so decided to begin exploring the local charity shops. At first she would search Urban Outfitters and Topshop websites each month to get a sense of the latest trends, and then would hit the charity shops to find similar second hand wear. But the more she shopped, the more she developed her own sense of style. She began to steer away from high street names, to create a wardrobe described in her own words as 'eclectic, punk grandma' style – every day was a different look. As she became more aware of the ethical and environmental costs of high street brands, she also became more inspired to find sustainable alternatives.

Fashion, the environment and veganism

Throughout college and university and for a few years after, Rachelle worked in the Body Shop in Preston. It was here that she really got to understand how conscious consumerism impacts the planet. She was very inspired by the work of Body Shop founder Anita Roddick, and fully integrated her environmental and social ethos into her life from then on. 'I think we should do as much for the planet as we can while we are on it', she says, and so she has adapted her lifestyle over the last few years to become as eco-friendly as possible.

After accumulating masses of junk throughout her adult life, Rachelle realized that she doesn't get happiness from things. She now tries to minimize her waste inspired by the idea of a 'zero waste lifestyle', which means she aims to reduce the amount of rubbish she produces. Every year in Britain each household produces over 1 tonne of rubbish, and the long-term effects of overproducing plastic, overusing many fossil fuels and destroying our natural habitat are only just beginning to surface. Soon there might be an urgent need for us all to adopt a zero waste lifestyle as it seems increasingly necessary to reduce our use of resources to ensure the future survival of our planet. She says 'if you cut the crap from your life you're not worrying about all the clutter amassing around you, or feeling guilty about putting out wheelie bins full of landfill each week. Plus instead of spending money on materialistic things you buy smart, out of a sustainable material that at the end of its life can be recycled or composted'. Rachelle also became a vegan two years ago, primarily to stop funding animal cruelty, and align her diet with her ethics. So she now eats a meat and dairy free diet, buys makeup and cosmetic products that avoid animal cruelty, as well as finding possible alternatives from dominant high street fashion labels.

As it is for many young people, buying a house and getting on the housing ladder is extremely challenging for Rachelle. So after living and working in Preston and Lancaster for eight years she now lives in a little caravan on the drive of her parents' new house in Cark-in-Cartmel. Always an optimist she has used this as an opportunity to simplify her life, and gave away and sold a lot of her things, catalysing her zero waste lifestyle. From here she works on her fashion career, writing fashion pages for a variety of magazines and on her own blog 'Inspired by the Retired'.

'I think it's difficult to get a career in the area unless you're interested in hospitality or agriculture. There's not a huge demand for fashion stylists', Rachelle jokes. Her move from Preston was a brave one, after finishing university many of her classmates moved to London, but she chose to return to her country roots and pursue a career in fashion from there. Luckily in the days of the internet you can forge a freelance career in fashion writing from just about anywhere, so now Rachelle is able to combine her love for the countryside with fashion. Her fashion blog acts as a platform to encourage other young people to live an eco-friendly lifestyle, and what's more it tells you how you can achieve it in style.

Sweeney Bobs of Cartmel

-

A day in the life of the local barber

'It was a bright and sunny day, not unusual for the Cartmel Peninsula. With seating arranged, shaving foam at the ready and cut-throat razors sharpened, husband and wife team, Paul and Phillipa Longster awaited the onslaught of eager customers.

The first of many clients took to the famous reclining seat, hoping not to be dropped down through the trap door to be made into Mrs Lovett's meat pies. A large, unshaven customer took to the seat, he was instantly lathered up and the sharp razor glided across his chin cutting down the bristles with ease. Paul (the barber) caught a glimpse of a well-dressed gentleman staring through the glass window. He watched for a while and after entered the shop. He exclaimed, "I am really impressed with how you use that razor with such accuracy, it looks like an amazing experience".

He then went on to explain that he was the fashion designer Ted Baker, and stated he was going to send us a new range of products. Three days later Ted was good to his word, and a huge box of shaving products arrived. It just shows that you never know just who is watching in Cartmel!'

Written by Paul Longster.

Philipa Longster and barber preparing the scissors for a busy day ahead

Billy and Mick Shaw

-

One dog and his man

It's that time, it's that time again! Tail wagging, I follow my Dad, Mick, in excitement as he reaches up to get my lead just in time for our early morning walk. I jump at him repeatedly in glee, whimpering with each extended leap up as he bends down and fumbles over me to clip it on, I don't know why it takes him so long. We proudly accompany each other out, Mick even opens the door for me - he is courteous like that. We follow the same route each morning through the village greeting each of our neighbours we pass, as we make our way to the racecourse. It is spring and the hedgerows are lined with beautiful wild flowers and the sweet aroma fills our nostrils - must be the handiwork of those Cartmel in Bloom people again. The grass is long, green and thick on the racecourse grounds and on the horizon I can hear the beckoning call of the tall and ever-growing trees.

I love our daily quests, the freedom I feel as Mick unclips my lead, and wind once again rushes through my fur when I make my way towards the trees in search of the those quick-stepping squirrels. Together Mick and I walk down a meandering path following the twist and turn of the river, in search of the day's adventures. Mick reverently sticks to the tracks, slowly plodding along, but I make the most of my freedom and bounce through the forest in search of sticks. Occasionally, we stumble across an old friend or make a new one, both human and dog. We have a little chat and play for a while until we part ways, returning to our own paths. I do enjoy making new friends with visitors to the village, and greet each one with the same enthusiasm. Some of the new doggies can sometimes be aggressive, but that is their problem, not mine - I just leave them to it. Sometimes, I do prefer

Billy and his owner Mick

my human friends who I can always rely on for attention and the occasional treat.

As Mick calls me closer I bound towards him, and as he reattaches my lead I know we are heading to the next stop on our morning escapades, the local pub. We are regulars, and pop in every day for a pint or two, using the opportunity to catch up with the daily gossip and have a chat with the locals. My favourites are the ones that present me with treats and attention, especially Terry who always has something yummy in his pocket for me. I like to sit upright, which some people think is strange, I'm not sure why as I like to sit upright with the humans. I have often been caught on camera with a pint in front of me, much to the amusement of visitors.

Mick Shaw

My father is a large and gentle man, he has short grey hair and wears a blue fleece and a white checked shirt. He is a happy, easy-going chap, with a good sense of humour. He always makes little jokes that he finds hilarious, but I'm not sure the other villagers agree, though they love him nonetheless and he is a key part of the local community. He started to visit Cartmel ten years ago with Katrina my mum (his wife) who has been coming to the village for over 30 years. He immediately fell in love with the place and they moved here soon after. Now he is enjoying the slow-paced retired life in Cartmel, after building up his own furniture frame company in Nottinghamshire for over forty years.

Before I came Mick didn't think he wanted a dog, but after a couple of years of nagging and persuasion from Katrina, he decided to go and take a look. I was the last dog in the litter, all my brothers and sisters had gone and I was beginning to feel all alone, then Mick walked in and it was love at first sight. We have been inseparable ever since and you will rarely see one of us without the other. Come rain or shine, we follow our village route. The other locals joke that when it has snowed you always know when we have been there because of the distinctive tracks we leave on the ground.

Mick Shaw

The famous Billy Border

I have become a bit of a celebrity in the village in recent years. Villagers and visitors adore my quirky ways, and all want to take my picture. I even have my own Facebook page where I keep in touch with people and keep them posted on our escapades. As the visitors return many of them ask where I am. It is hard for me to remember everyone, but I make sure I remember the ones with the treats and run over to them in excitement when I catch a waft of a mouth-watering scent. There is always something exciting happening in Cartmel, someone to give me attention, something new to smell, or chase, or chew. I am free to frolic through the woods with Mick, or even go to the local pub for a pint, I couldn't ask for anything more. It's a dog's life, you know!

Jean and Howard Johns

-

Founders of the pudding that conquered the world

As the bell rings and the door opens, a warm sweet smell sweeps the air. As the fledgling puddings protected in shiny silver armour brave the world for the first time, they march four by four out of the oven ready to take on the day. Once cooled they are taken to six kind ladies all dressed in long white coats and black and white checked hats who individually dress each pudding using a large ladle. They scoop down into a bucket filled with the famous Cartmel Sticky Toffee Pudding sauce and dress each one with a quick flick of the wrist. Once set, the puddings now embark on their journey as their shiny armour is sealed, and they are packed into a brightly coloured sleeve. As the parade of the puddings comes to an end, they assemble for their final inspection before leaving home for good.

From humble beginnings

Cartmel Sticky Toffee Pudding has become a world-renowned, award-winning pudding, acclaimed by the likes of David Cameron, Madonna, Elton John and chef Jean-Christophe Novelli who said that Cartmel Sticky Toffee Pudding was 'definitely the best in the world'. It is sold in national chain shops across the UK including Waitrose, Booths, Sainsbury's, Selfridges and more, and has become one of the most sought-after of sticky toffee puddings. This might seem unusual for a small medieval village in the rural Lake District, but take one mouthful of the moist, date-stuffed sponge softened by a rich toffee sauce and you will understand why. The pudding came from humble origins and was first developed in 1989, the year the founders Jean

Jean and Howard Johns　　　　©Cartmel Sticky Toffee Pudding

and Howard Johns took over what was then the village post office.

The couple have just celebrated their golden wedding anniversary, and like any good marriage, the ascent of Cartmel Sticky Toffee Pudding was also created through love, hard labour, and long-lasting dedication. It is these unified organic elements that set the pudding apart from other desserts, giving it an authenticity that originated at the hands of a family business. In order to satisfy the appetite of the local residents and passing holidaymakers Jean and her young daughter Sarah used to experiment with different recipes inside the post office. They worked together to create homemade cakes, pies, ready meals and, of course, sticky toffee pudding for the shop.

The post office, located in Cartmel Square, was well-situated, surrounded by the local pubs and the racecourse, so that people often passed and caught a waft of that now famous sweet scent. It was this alluring aroma that enticed punters and set in motion the unstoppable popularity of the pudding. As the summer tourists returned home, the post office phone was bombarded with enquiries about where else they could buy the pudding before they returned again in April. For Jean and Howard Johns, this was an epiphany, the sudden realisation that what they made in their small corner store had huge potential. Filled with passion and ambition they embarked upon their mission, and took samples of their pudding to other parts of the Lake District, Yorkshire and Lancashire, and it was from here that their business began to take off.

Jean and Howard Johns

The couple have lived in Cartmel most of their married life (50 years), and have always played a major role in the local community. Both took part in community activities, Howard was a bell ringer at the Cartmel Priory Church, their children sang in the local choir, and attended both Cartmel primary and secondary schools. In 1971 they took over the Kings Arms pub, one of two pubs located in the village square, and spent thirteen years building up the restaurant and immersing themselves in village life. The pubs are really where you find your place in Cartmel, the hub of local activity, gossip and at times out and out debauchery; they are places to truly get to know one another. It was during this time, running a pub, that they fell in love with Cartmel and became part of the community.

Staying in the hospitality sector they left the Kings Arms and temporarily left Cartmel to open the At Home restaurant in Grange-over-Sands, which remains open to this day, under different ownership, as one of the favourite dining places in Grange. But the magnetic pull of Cartmel again drew them in and they returned in 1989 to develop their sticky toffee pudding, as they transformed the village post office into what is now Cartmel Village Shop.

The growth of an empire

As the demand for Cartmel Sticky Toffee Pudding grew, the couple ran out of space in the kitchen of the post office, and relocated to Wellknowe Farmhouse in 2000, where they continued to keep the business close to home. In the vast area surrounding the house they had more room to expand, and designed and built a multi-purpose kitchen in their garden. The new kitchen was completed in 2000, and opened up new possibilities to further cement the business' reputation as makers of one of the UK's most loved puddings. As the business developed the couple needed to bring in outside help in order to meet the demand and ensure it maintained a competitive and unique edge. This included Charlotte Sharphouse who has a keen eye for business and was instrumental in developing the brand of Cartmel Sticky Toffee Pudding for many years. She has recently left to focus more on her and her husband's expanding business at Old Hall Farm in Bouth.

Working together they approached Waitrose, who grabbed the opportunity to stock the pudding in their stores down South. With this new deal secured, the business snowballed and soon they had outgrown their garden kitchen. By 2004, a kitchen four times as big was built on land they bought in the neighbouring village Flookburgh – which continues to be the home of Cartmel Sticky Toffee Pudding to this day. The old post office was transformed into the Cartmel Village Shop, an old-fashioned food store stocking all kinds of fine foods including, of course, their own sticky toffee pudding. The recipe, and the way the pudding is made, still remains unchanged, as everything continues to be done by hand. They have continued to develop and experiment, and now have a whole variety of puddings available, but the original still remains the most popular by far.

At home in Cartmel

Cartmel has a huge place in the hearts of Jean and Howard Johns. Since living there they have witnessed it transform into a hub of fine cuisine. The arrival of Michelin-starred chef Simon Rogan, the development of Unsworth's Yard with its brewery, cheese shop and wine shop, and several pubs in the village serving good food, have enticed new visitors to the village. It was the place they raised their children, who would frolic through the woods and park, by the old river and the old graveyard. It is an idyllic place to raise a family free from fear, in the safe grasp of nature. It was the whole family who worked together to bring Cartmel Sticky Toffee Pudding into the world, and it continues to be nurtured by the family to this day. Though Jean and Howard have both taken a step back from the business, it has been passed down the line. Their daughter Sarah and husband David now run the Cartmel Village Shop, and their son, Simon, runs the bakery. Even their young grandchildren Elizabeth and Frederick both help out in the shop from time to time.

As the mixers continue whirling, Cartmel Sticky Toffee Pudding continues to fill the stomachs of hundreds of thousands of people each year. Handmade with love, care and dedication, it really is the pudding that has conquered the world.

Tracey Webb

Tending to her duties inside The Larchtree Cartmel

Michael Bates

Tending to his allotment on Cartmel Racecourse

Reverend Nick Devenish and the Priory Church

-

A significant place of welcome

A s the ancient clock of the Priory Church chimes ten the village is already bustling on a crisp Sunday morning. Bar staff from the three pubs around the Square throw open their doors, and put up their daily signs in order to tempt those who pass by to sample their local ales. Billy and Mick greet them as they slowly plod through the village, heading back from the racecourse following their morning stroll. They walk over the small, stone bridge passing David Unsworth who walks around attentively checking that all is in order in his yard, his concentration intermittently broken as he glances up to greet people as they pass. This morning these include a collection of bell-ringers who hurry past on their way to attend to their morning duties. One-by-one the bell-ringers appear inside the church porch, rubbing their hands together to keep warm while they wait for the whole group to arrive.

Once together they embark on a hair-raising but awe-inspiring journey up to the bell tower, an ancient place at one of the highest points of the Priory. The chief bell-ringer takes the lead, walking the red carpet, past the long wooden aisles to the back of the church. Together they follow in the footsteps of thousands of monks and worshippers who have taken this route for hundreds of years leading up to this moment. In single file they make their way down a long dark corridor, at the end of which sits a small wooden door. Like a scene from *Alice in Wonderland*, the chief slowly lifts his hand to push open the small door to unveil a narrow and winding stone spiral staircase. Heads ducked, they squeeze through the door and carefully climb the staircase placing one foot cautiously in front of the other. Once at the top they are presented with their final challenge – the balcony – a long narrow

The Reverend Nick Devenish inside the Priory Church

passage on top of the church in an open space where the railing sits just over your hips. As each one passes in turn, cold air rushes past their ears and they take a moment to breathe in the vast green views spanning across the village and beyond.

Inside, the bell-ringers take hold of six long, thick red ropes that drop down from the ceiling and begin to pull in turn. With each movement the bells begin to awaken from their wooden axes, and sway further with the effort of each pull, creating a chorus of ringing that echoes across the village letting people know that it is time to come and worship.

In the village below, sunshine warmly greets the congregation as they arrive for their Sunday morning service. They softly chatter amongst themselves as they take their pews and prepare to praise God. The service commences and a procession led by The Reverend Nick Devenish ceremoniously enters the church. The Servers and the Choir fall in behind and slowly step to the distinct and awe-inspiring sound of the organ, which sets the scene, leading the congregation in the morning hymn. In this ancient house a sense of calm and belonging sweeps over the congregation as they come together to practice traditional Christian worship. Loud hymns echo in the rafters, and moments of still prayer form space for collective meditation for thoughts and reflections on our time. At the end of the service each member takes part in the Holy Communion (sharing of bread and wine), and row-by-row they make their way to the front of the church altar, passing the intricately carved medieval wooden choir benches on their way up. In groups they kneel down to receive a blessing, bread and wine. This tradition ends with a reflective prayer, final hymn and closing procession of the Priest, Servers and the Choir.

Church clock chimes – moving with the times

Cartmel Priory has always been the heart of the village, an ancient jewel, proudly towering over the inhabitants for over 800 years. Just like all remaining churches of its time it has a long and illustrious history, but it is unique for its size in such a small village. Most churches with its history and grandeur are found in cities or large towns. The Priory has been compared to prestigious places like Durham Cathedral or York Minster, and this legacy can only be attributed to one man, the founder of the Priory, Sir William

Marshal.

Records show that Sir Marshal was awarded land in Cartmel in 1187, on which he founded the Priory Monastery in 1189. He was a significant man of his era, and rose up through the hierarchies of society, to become one of history's notable knights and a close ally of King Henry III. He built the Priory primarily as a monastery but also stipulated that it would act as a Parish Church to provide space for the local community to worship. It was this condition that later saved the Priory from destruction at the dissolution of the monasteries by the notorious Henry VIII in 1537. When the royal officials ventured armed and ready to take over the Priory and its possessions the local Parish fought back, they claimed that this was more than a monastery it was also their place of worship, and for that reason it should be spared. This resistance was inspired by the Pilgrimage of Grace, the rising which started in Yorkshire against Henry VIII's break with the Roman Catholic Church, and because of this their concerns were relayed back to the authorities and the church was spared.

In the years to follow the Priory survived insurgent attacks from the Scottish invaders, Henry VIII, Oliver Cromwell's troops (the bullet holes from this battle still remain on the wooden door of the church), dilapidation and renovation, World War I, World War II and more. All this time the church provided a place of daily worship, welcome and belonging for the people who reside and visit the Cartmel Peninsula.

Where we belong – The church, the people and the Reverend

Since the inauguration of the Cartmel Priory Church, Cartmel has become a historic place of welcome. The monastic enclosure that was built during the founding of the church still runs through the village, and has been used to form part of the walls for houses now over 300 years old. It is this ancient spine that has made Cartmel and the Priory a destination of pilgrimage for hundreds of years. Even before the railway was constructed to connect across Morecombe Bay, pilgrims dutifully trekked over the Sands to visit the church. Some even lost their lives to quicksand or changing tides in the process; the remains of a select few are buried in the Priory graveyard.

Today, when interest in the church and Christianity is waning, particularly amongst young people, one cannot help but observe the central role the Priory church continues to play in the village of Cartmel. Whether for Christian worship with packed services, or a cultural and historical visiting site, it has created a sense of welcome in the village both spiritually and communally and this has attracted people searching for belonging for centuries. For Rev'd Nick Devenish and many others like him this is what first attracted him to Cartmel and the Priory.

Like many people in the UK, Nick never attended church as a child, and initially had no intention to change this. He pursued a career in retail as a commercial manager for Marks & Spencer - a demanding role where you drive sales and boost their brand. Little did he know, as he lay in bed one Sunday morning, that his life was about to change and take a completely new direction. It was in the lead-up to Christmas, when his wife turned to him and said that she didn't want her son to grow up thinking that Christmas was about what you're going to get, so she wanted to take him to church to make sure he knew its true meaning. At this point in his life, Nick didn't really see the point in going to church, but wanted to please his wife, so he reluctantly clambered out of bed to accompany her and their son to their local parish church.

On his approach he felt like his morning off had been stolen, and now he had to spend it in a cold and empty church filled with old people. But the service contradicted all his expectations: the congregation filled the hall, and as soon as he entered the church he was made to feel welcome. He felt that this was a place where he could belong. This experience completely changed his perception and because of that they went back, and kept going back.

After several years Nick left his job at Marks & Spencer and found his calling in the church instead. It took ten years of learning about different denominations, branching out to explore ones beyond the walls of his local parish church and observing the variety of ways Christian worship is undertaken across the country. After ten years he was finally ordained as a vicar and he has never looked back - he had found the community of which he could be a part.

Cartmel Priory

Like most people who fall in love with or move to the Lake District, Nick Devenish spent many years coming on holiday to Hawks Head. He had never heard of Cartmel until the job vacancy opened at the Priory and he decided to pay a visit. He immediately fell in love with the church, applied for the job and was appointed in January 2012. Nick sensed that there is still a strong role for the vicar within the community of Cartmel. This is something that has been lost in many other villages across the UK, including Nick's previous place of work where he had spent a number of years building a new church and attempted to rebuild a congregation from scratch. Cartmel was a place where he felt he could make a real difference.

The future of Cartmel and the role of the church for the next generation is unknown. With increasing apathy shown towards Christian religion amongst the younger generation, and the changing demographics of the village, will the Priory always remain as Sir William Marshal had intended - a place for the local people - or will it become a place only occasionally visited by those who pass through? For now though, it is still very much alive, and is in the safe hands of Rev'd Nick Devenish, striving toward and succeeding in his mission of making it a place of welcome for all.

Jimmy Moffatt

-

The village horse whisperer

'And they're off, racing for the William Hill Trophy Handicap Chase, three miles and half a furlong in front of the field. They're on the first of nineteen fences, and Chief Dan George and Razor Royal are among the first to show. Bensalem made a mistake at the very first, right in the middle of the field, as they head on towards the second jump. Joe Lively has settled down in front, and of course Specialist leading from Comply or Die in the red cap. Chief Dan George wider out with Stan on the outer of Razer Royal as they turn to the next fences which are three, four and five, plain water and open dips. Joe Lively leading the field, Chief Dan George and Beat the Boys are wider as they take fence number three, Chief Dan George not as fluent as some there. On towards the water jump, Chief Dan George and Comply or Die are the ones that are in the lead, but still a long, long way to go. The Package remains two thirds of the ways back through, as they approach another open ditch, and Comply and Die who is leading now. We lose No Where there who brings down Exmoor Ranger, who brings down Casey Jones. Exmoor Ranger and Casey Jones both put out of the race by No Where's departure so three of them are out of the contest at that fence, as they begin the turn downhill…'

'The order as they set out on the final circuit: Comply or Die in the red cap on the stand side of Joe Lively, Chief Dan George right faced towards the out of Stan in the blue and pink, Razel Royal in the stripes; Ogee towards the inner of Niche Market and Offshore Account in the pale colours. Bensalem is getting closer, a juddering mistake by Kicks for Free at the rear of the field. The Package is in the same position he was in a circuit or so ago with about four or five behind still travelling comfortably…'

'As they turn back for home, Ogee on the inside of Chief Dan George and Offshore Account, they go in three in line they go towards the final fence. The Package, and Niche Market take the last fence, Ogee got in a bit tight. Chief Dan George within half a length now, then The Package, on the outside is Offshore Account. Up the hill Chief Dan George wearing down Oh-G about a neck in it, here comes The Package in second place. The Package is absolutely flying as they hit the line, but CHIEF DAN GEORGE beats The Package in the William Hill. Flying in at third Ogee, in fourth Offshore Account. In a traditional theatrical moment, Chief Dan George and Paddy Aspell have won the William Hill Trophy here for the Jimmy Moffat Stable, great Northern win!' (commentary taken from William Hill Trophy Handicap Chase 2010).

Jimmy Moffatt, a dark-haired, short, unassuming man, dressed casually in a blue Gillet and a Panama hat, sits opposite me looking down into his tea as he relives this emotional win. The Cheltenham Festival is one the highlights of the jump season, host to tough competition as the jockeys, owners, trainers, punters, bookmakers and horses all battle for one of the highest racing honours of the year. In 2010, one of Jimmy's horses, Chief Dan George took the prestigious cup, during a close finish in which he took the lead just at the right moment.

Jimmy is touted as one of the leading horse trainers in the area, and just had a winner at Cartmel races on Monday of the week I met with him. In addition to this win, he got married the week before, and I get a sense that he is overwhelmed with emotion as I begin to ask him about his life as a leading horse trainer, husband and former jockey.

'Riding and training is in my blood' he explained. 'My great-grandfather, grandfather and father were all trainers, and my mother and father met in a yard where my father was a trainer, so I was born into racing […]. I sat on my first horse at the age of three, so I have never known anything else'. Jimmy owns his own training stables in Cartmel – James Moffatt Racing Stables – where he works to develop his practices as a leading horse trainer, with over 30 horses currently on his books. He follows in the footsteps of his father Dudley Moffatt, also a leading racehorse trainer, who originally built

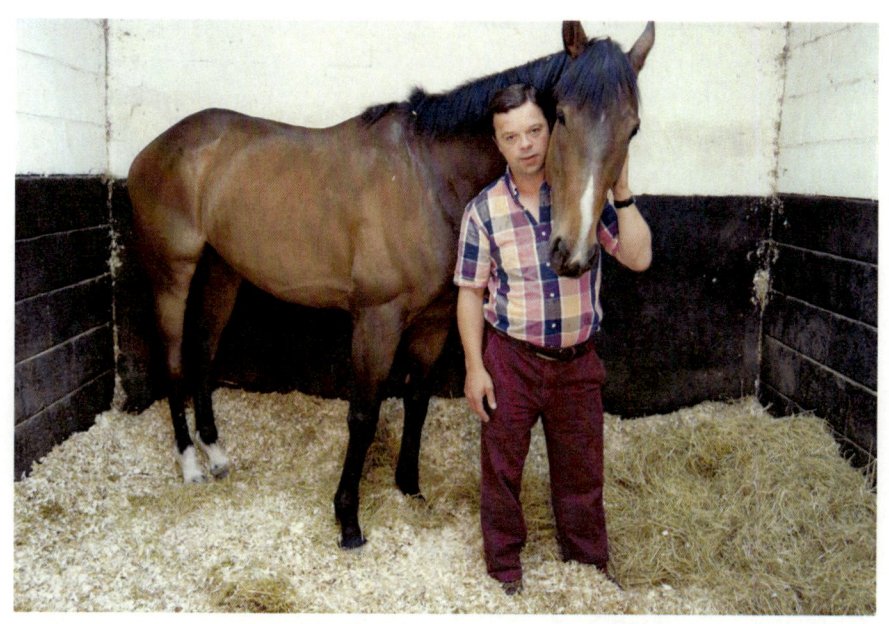

Jimmy Moffatt with his horse Altruism

the stables. Jimmy took over the license in 2003 and has since worked to modernise and reinvent the training ground.

Jimmy was 12 when his dad took over the training ground in Cartmel, and by then he had already mastered the art of riding, and began to jump and gallop by the time he was 13. In 1988 at the age of 16 he travelled to Ireland to be an apprentice jockey to renowned jockey Tommy Stack. Stack is best known for riding the legendary steeplechaser Red Rum into his record third Grand National triumph, so a young Jimmy was learning his trade from some of the best in the business.

Following training, Jimmy had his first ride as a jockey in Ayr in Scotland in 1989, he won his first race and lost his second, so experienced both ends of the spectrum. 'At 16 I thought I was going to be the best in the business! Then I began to put on weight, so someone suggested I become a jump jockey instead' Jimmy explains, chuckling nostalgically. He returned to England in 1990 and started riding jumps. He achieved great things during his 14-year racing career riding 78 winners, including The County Hurdle at Cheltenham Festival, The Scottish Champion Hurdle and The West Yorkshire Hurdle. In 2003 Jimmy turned his attention to training. He wanted to work behind the scenes and create the winners, rather than ride them.

As a trainer he has now trained over 109 winners. He claimed his 100th winner when Altruism triumphed at Cartmel races in 2015. Yet despite training hundreds of horses, Chief Dan George has a special place in his heart, he was Jimmy's first grade one winner at Aintree and Cheltenham, both described as life-changing wins. Chief Dan George was owned by Maurice Chapman - a local self-made man - who rose from a council estate to being awarded an MBE for his services to British exports. 'Sadly Chapman died on my birthday in 2014' Jimmy explains. 'He was doing what he loved, herding his sheep with his family around him'. Maurice left Chief Dan to Jimmy. A stubborn and independent-minded horse, he has not let anyone ride him since his last win two and a half years ago. Chief Dan is now enjoying his final years in a fifty-acre field with a stream running through it, bought for him by his loving owner Maurice before he died.

©James Moffatt

Where is the heart in such a controversial sport?

The controversial world of horse racing has come under heavy criticism in recent years. NGOs and animal rights activists want to see an end to commercial racing, describing it as a brutal and exploitative industry, through which 200 thoroughbreds die per year. Jockey Ruby Walsh's comment 'you can replace a horse' following the death of his horse Our Conor at Cheltenham in 2014, only served to reinforce views of horse racing as a heartless sport.

      Riding horses dates back hundreds, even thousands, of years in Britain. The practice was brought here by the Romans who organized the first competitions around 200A.D., but it more than likely started well before this time. From the skill of the jockey, to the cachet of the breed, to the rush of cheering them on, horseracing is the second biggest spectator sport in the country. Throughout history the trajectory of horse racing has been influenced by royalty, including King Henry VIII and Charles I who both set breeding laws and standardized rules building the sport's importance in the UK's national heritage. Today horse racing is still known as a regal sport, even Queen Elizabeth II owned horses that went on to win at Royal Ascot and other races. Yet despite its high standing, through gambling, newspapers and television horse racing is still accessible to the masses.

What is the reality? Do owners and trainers really just see their horses as money making machines, or is there a heart in the sport? When talking to Jimmy Moffat it was clear that his heart is in it. His racehorses are pampered athletes fed quality hay, handmade and specially steamed to remove dust that could affect their lungs. They are exercised and trained daily and tucked in with a blanket at night. In Jimmy's own words: 'I would rather spend more on feeding one of my horses each week, than I do on myself'. Every horse has individual needs and requirements, and he needs to work out the right routine and nutrition to ensure that they are well-fed and looked after. As a trainer Jimmy has to work hard to get inside their heads, build trust and to find out what makes them tick. They are athletes so to get the best out of them you have to put a lot in. 'If you don't put everything you have into the horses, if you cut corners and don't give it your best, then there is someone else who will have and you will find that out publicly on the track', Jimmy emphasizes passionately.

Every year there are 672 UK-based trainers doing the same thing, giving all they have to develop and train their premium horses. So to maintain his competitive edge Jimmy has taken all the knowledge of his ancestors, lessons from people who trained and worked with him when he was younger, and also knowledge of different cultural practices of horse racing, and he has used all this as a foundation to build and develop his own style of training. Each year he works to maintain a competitive edge by investing in expanding his yard, but he believes that his main strength is that his heart goes into everything he does with his horses. 'For me', he explains, 'it is not about the money, my main motivation is difficult to quantify, it's the adrenaline rush you get when a horse wins, and seeing the joy on the owners' faces afterwards. It's working with the girls in the yard that look after them so well, and the feeling the team gets when you know you've done your job properly'.

Cartmel Home base

Jimmy is firmly rooted in Cartmel, he went to school in the village and grew up around horses in his dad's stables, so racing in Cartmel means a lot to him.

Over the last couple of years he has married and settled, which he describes as the best thing he has ever done, and it has helped to keep him focused and grounded in his home base. Jimmy and his wife have had their first son, Jenson James, who has just sat on his first racehorse Altruism (who recently broke the track record at Cartmel), at just four months old.

Each year, at the time of the races, Jimmy transforms from an unassuming and unnoticed grafter to a local celebrity when the races come to Cartmel. After his 2015 win, the local paper *Cartmel Racecourse* wrote:

> Local trainer James Moffatt proved the star of the season at Cartmel in 2015 with a fantastic year at the track to finish top trainer for the first time. A tearful Moffatt collected the Andrea Robinson Memorial Trophy at the final meeting of the eight-day Cartmel season after beating top Irish trainer Gordon Elliott, the four-times winner Donald McCain and Northern powerhouse Mickey Hammond to the title (Cartmel Racecourse website 2015).

Despite all his achievements, Jimmy remains a humble Cartmel character, he is never complacent, always working to develop and improve his winning formulas, putting his all into his training practices.

Jonathan Garratt

-

Racecourse director and pony enthusiast

Cars queue in lines through the village, stretching back from the racecourse, over the bridge, round the corner and past the church. Car-boots are filled with picnic baskets, tents, windbreaks, umbrellas (just in case) and copious amounts of wine and beer for the day of celebrations ahead. They slowly edge closer towards their destination, coordinated by traffic managers dressed in bright yellow vests calmly waving them through. It sets a scene similar to a well-choreographed dance-piece in which each performer takes it in turn to exit the stage, but in this performance they disappear through the racecourse gates. Pedestrians scatter, weaving around the cars, tractors and other people, as the first race of the day is underway - the race to get in.

Amongst the chaos, the pubs prepare for the onslaught of punters who descend on them in between the racing. Bar staff drag kegs of beer over the cobbles between the Royal Oak and the Kings Arms, and take a few deep breaths as they place the advertisement signs out, preparing themselves for the most profitable day of the year.

As they make their way in, attendees are split between the paddock side for the racing enthusiasts, and the course side for those who have come for a day of family fun. Historically these divides would have been along class lines - with lords and ladies in the paddock and everyone else in the course. But today in Cartmel people are not separated according to their classes: all different strata of society make their way through. Some are dressed in expensive thick tweed jackets and trousers, with blue shirts and finely polished shoes ready for a day of betting. Others are gearing up for celebratory drinks in brightly coloured dresses with large feathered hats and

Jonathan Garratt on Cartmel Racecourse

stiletto heels. Grandparents, parents and children come together year after year to enjoy picnics, family time and the occasional bet. The children make the most of the theme park, playing on the large slides, spinning around on the waltzers, and eating large amounts of candyfloss.

The layout of Cartmel Racecourse makes it one of the most unique racecourses in the UK, as elsewhere audiences are on the periphery of the course. Here, audiences are sat in the middle, in the heart of the ring and, as the tapes rise, the horses fly off and encircle the spectators who cheer in excitement as they pass.

The artistic director – Jonathan Garratt

At the centre of all this activity is Jonathan Garratt. He holds the artistic vision behind the festival of events and coordinates everything from his high tower. From here he watches his vision unfold in front of him. He sees the joy of the crowd, the galloping hooves and the fairground fun, all the time directing the performance, seeing his hard work turning into a reality.

Since coming to Cartmel over six years ago, Jonathan has invested a lot of time and effort into improving the quality of the racecourse. He has increased the number of annual meetings from three to four, so that there are now nine race days and sixty-three races in each season. This has expanded the races from two one-off events to a year-round calendar, and because of this he has been able to justify increased investment in the appearance of the course. Jonathan has also secured the services of highly acclaimed musicians including Jools Holland and the band Simply Red, all increasing the exposure of the Cartmel Race as both an event and a race day.

But as we sit talking, it becomes apparent that Jonathan is proudest of the new improvements that might not be immediately visible to the eye. As we know from Jimmy Moffatt's story, racehorses are athletes and need top conditions in order to perform at their best. So over the last few years Jonathan has made considerable efforts to improve the condition of the track. 'We have now developed a good root depth so that turf is able to drain more freely, and maintain a springy composition – which is every racer's dream. Horses need a solid surface, with some cushion to break the impact of their hooves. Cartmel is now able to provide this, and as a result a higher calibre of horse is coming to race in Cartmel than in previous years', Jonathan explains as we sit in the grandstand offices. You can tell that someone is passionate about their job and has good attention to detail when they start discussing the quality of soil and irrigation systems.

From a young age Jonathan knew he wanted a career working in racing. 'At the age of 16 the mother of a girlfriend asked, "what are you going to do with your life?" and I replied, "I want to run a racecourse" which is quite an unusual thing for a 16-year-old to say I suppose', Jonathan reminisces. Born on a farm in Kent, he grew up riding ponies and it was this that sparked his passion and love for horse racing. After graduating with a degree in agriculture he began to do odd jobs at racecourses, and at one point he even rode in amateur races. 'I finished fifth in the point-to-point Ashford Valley Hunt Members race in 1986', he says, gesturing to a picture of himself on the wall. A humble chap, he uses this experience to inspire younger generations by explaining that he might not have been the best jockey, but he found another way in, and if you want to work in a sector badly enough - you can find a way to make it happen.

Pursuing his dreams, Jonathan became the Director of Fontwell Park until 2003. When he left he changed direction; rather than focusing on running one racecourse, he moved to Scotland and worked for Scottish Racing – an organisation which acts as a cooperative on behalf of the five Scottish racecourses. After six years he started to get itchy feet and decided that it was time for a new challenge, and wanted to go back to managing one specific track. But he didn't just want any racecourse, he wanted one that still made an event out of the day, one that wasn't solely focused on the racing and betting – and so he found Cartmel. 'Not every race day in the country is run to attract a large crowd. Many racecourses run lots and lots of races, but don't attract a large audience. Usually this is because their main revenue is generated through betting and broadcast rights'. Interestingly, out of all the jump tracks in the UK, Cartmel is the third best attended in the country, after Aintree and Cheltenham. Jonathan came to Cartmel to continue the long history of the races here and to build up the event.

Cartmel Racecourse – A brief history

The grounds in Cartmel have been used as a racecourse since the village was a monastery. The monks were enthusiastic jockeys and rode donkeys and then later progressed to horses. Legend has it that they were so dedicated to their sport that when the Bishop of York made the death-defying journey across Morecambe Bay, he was disappointed to find that there was no delegation of monks to greet him on his arrival. Quite angry, the Bishop of York later discovered that the reason for this was that all the monks were racing in the park at the time.

This informal race gathering continued for many years and developed into a festival for the locals, with wrestling and a hound trail in the 1600-1700s. In 1856 the first Cartmel race meeting was properly formalised. Back then, racing only took place once a year on Whit Monday, and this continued right up until it was suspended during World War I and II. It was only later revived with large investments from local landowners and wealthy families who restored the course to its former glory. This investment meant that a Saturday was added in 1947. At this time the racecourse was only used by amateur jockeys and very few professionals attended. It wasn't until the 1960s that the racecourse began to professionalise, and due to the increased success another date was added to the racing calendar in August. The races were then held in May and August for many years, until a date was added in July around fifteen years ago. Now there are races in May, June, July and August.

The racecourse is owned by the Holker Estate. Lord Cavendish, an enthusiastic racegoer and Chairman of the racecourse, has invested a lot of time into the management of the course over the last few decades. This investment has ensured the future of racing at Cartmel. And as we now know, the course has continued to improve under the management of Jonathan Garratt.

Cartmel is a unique racecourse situated in such close proximity to a medieval village. Across the country races are held in a variety of locations, some in cities, others in open country, but it is very rare to be able to walk out of the racecourse and into a village square in a matter of minutes. This location sets Cartmel Racecourse apart from other courses, with attendees going to the local pubs in between races, and then walking back over to the course to continue enjoying the racing. This is the draw of Cartmel Races. It makes for the perfect location of a festival, and is one of the reasons so many people attend and completely transform the village each year.

Future of Cartmel racecourse

Cartmel Races is an important source of income for local businesses. It draws in crowds of up to 20,000 people to each event, most of whom spend time and money in the village, boosting local pubs, hotels, and other businesses and helping them to survive the long and quieter winter months. Unlike other areas of the village these crowds have little to do with Cartmel's recent fame, as they have been steadily growing for years.

Though the locals have many different opinions on the races, most are proud of it being a fixture in Cartmel. The races are very much rooted in the village heritage. For example, every year on the Sunday race day in August, a racehorse from Jimmy Moffatt's farm trots round to the Priory Church porch to be blessed by Rev'd Nick Devonish. Nick is also the chaplain to the racecourse and says a prayer blessing in the parade room before the racing commences. In keeping with supporting local businesses, each race is sponsored by local companies, including Cartmel Sticky Toffee Pudding, Willow Water, Furness Fish and Game and more. This gives it a local branding and distinguishes it from other courses that might be endorsed by a plethora of non-descript national and multinational corporations.

Just like many others who are interested in horseracing, Jonathan Garratt was attracted to Cartmel because of the racecourse. Although different from Cheltenham, Aintree or the other large racecourses that are havens for racing purists (with top jockeys, horses and events) Cartmel Racecourse offers something unique. 'Professional jockeys, racing enthusiasts and families are drawn back here time and time again because it is a fun event to attend and a special place to be', Jonathan concludes.

John Kerr

–

Cartmel's rare-book dealer

T he curfew tolls the knell of parting day,
 The lowing herd wind slowly o'er the lea,
The ploughman homeward plods his weary way,
 And leaves the world to darkness and to me.

Thomas Gray, 1751

This is the first stanza of the famous poem 'Elegy Written in a Country Churchyard' written in 1751 by the celebrated English poet Thomas Gray. Many editions of Gray's 'Elegy' have been published in the last couple of centuries, printed as elegant collector's editions, in magazines, incorporated into poetry books, and mass printed for schools across the UK who used the poem as a standard syllabus text for many decades. But in my pages you will find the entire original poem, the definitive version printed in 1768, and proofread by the poet himself. My spine is growing older now, my leather worn, but inside I'm still as crisp as I was the day I was printed. I'm proud that the elegant words of Gray have graced my pages for all these years. Though the world may have changed since Gray wrote his 'Elegy', the meaning behind his words has not lost its value. His dark, heavy meditation on death, views on remembrance and ponderings on the class struggles of the time still resonate with readers. With the turn of each decade as new fingers grace my pages, and new eyes scan his stanzas, each reader is once more swept up in these powerful words.

During the last two and a half centuries I have travelled far and wide across the UK. I have sat on shelves made of fine mahogany adorning the walls in the homes of lords and ladies, in vast libraries coloured by the spines of an array of literary masterpieces. I have been cast aside into boxes, and then re-found time and time again. In all that time I have had the privilege to be catalogued alongside other literary gems, each one imbued with the spirit of the times. I have been read at flamboyant soirees in the mansion houses of the 18th century, where the gentry drank fine wine, played piano and danced the night away. To quieter times in a children's nursery in the mid 19th century, watching as they fidget in a disobedient manner. I was packed in a suitcase and sheltered in boxes in the safety of the countryside during World War I and II, and lived to tell my tale. Each time I have taken note of the fashion, cuisine and changing architecture of the times.

'Going once, going twice, going three times… sold to the highest bidder! Hand the book to the man on the left with the blue jacket', shouts the auctioneer as my journey across the country continues. The gavel slams down, and I'm packaged up and taken over to my new owner. I wonder who and what awaits me this time?

Kerr and Sons - Books in the blood

Kerr and Sons Antiquarian Booksellers occupy two properties in Cartmel: The Gatehouse Bookshop just to the front of the medieval archway in the Square, and opposite the Vicarage at Priory Barn. Inside these quirky buildings, the shelves are lined with a beautiful range of leather, vellum and cloth-bound books, individually labelled, and carefully placed to tell a story of time gone by. Maps, classic poems and history books filled with stories and anecdotes of the British Empire and more, are stacked everywhere from the ground floor to the ceiling. Much the same as outside in Cartmel, the shops are a treasure trove of different times and events all in one place.

John Kerr is a tall and amiable man, and as we speak he tells me how his family has for almost a century dealt in antiquarian books. 'The business goes back to 1933, and it all started when my dad saw an advert for a typed list of books for sale on the Stockton and Darlington Railway. He went to buy them, sold them successfully for a profit and built the business up from there. He was a self-made man', John proudly claims. John's father, Norman Kerr, founded Kerr's Books in 1933 and together with his wife Paddy issued over 200 catalogues specialising in books on transport - ships, railways,

John Kerr and son Robert Kerr

aviation, motors and engineering. 'It was a different time then', John explains, 'to specialise gave you your edge, so anyone looking to find a transport book knew to come to them'.

Bookselling is in John's blood, he is the fifth generation bookseller on his mother's side and second generation on his father's side. Now he and his son Robert run Kerr's Books in Cartmel, which is going into its third generation of book selling. As we talk he pulls out books from the shelves surrounding us, opening up ancient maps, tales from history, and also the first collected edition of Thomas Gray's poems, including the 'Elegy Written in a Country Churchyard'. To reiterate its importance John begins to read the poem and finishes at the end of the first stanza. He had the book rebound locally after he bought it in the auction, ensuring that the leather spine and marbled paperboards were in keeping with the period in which it was first printed. This is true to the definition of an antiquarian book, something that was printed over 100 years ago, and kept in, or as near to as is possible, its original condition. It is selective buying like this that has kept Kerr's Books in business for all this time.

Although raised in the area and brought up surrounded by antiquarian books, for twenty years John took a different career in conservation, environmental planning and countryside management. In the late 1980s something drew him back to the family business and he began to help his father out part-time. Inspired by this work in late 2003 he decided to quit his job, move back to Cartmel and go full-time with the business. This period proved very important and he was fully involved in running the business before his father died in 2005.

Since then John has taken the business in a whole new direction, he sold the legacy of his father's transport stock, and followed in the footsteps of his uncles who were interested in a broader range of subjects. 'Today you can't focus on just one thing, like my father could [...], you have to diversify' John explains. Kerr and Sons have almost completely moved away from their focus on transport to acquire a more generalised stock. Now they trade in a wide range of antiquarian books mainly from the 18th, 19th and 20th centuries, including literature, poetry, natural history, topography, travel, mountaineering, field sports and of course the occasional transport book. Each book is on its own journey, and sometimes they contain notes, letters, or newspaper cuttings relevant to happenings of times gone by.

The future of Kerr's Books – antiquarian books in the digital age

The hunt is still on for antiquarian books, so in order to keep up with the demand the Kerr family attend auctions, trade fairs, the homes of private sellers and look online all in search of rare finds and collectors' items. 'The business has gone full circle', John explains as he continues to flick through the pages of Thomas Gray's book. 'My father was always a catalogue book seller, and now we sell the majority of our books online'. Trade in the shop is seasonal, or as John describes it 'the icing on the cake', and now most of their business is done via the internet. 'We do the same thing', John says, 'but now we pack them up and post them all around the world'. Through the internet Kerr's Books sell between 50-100 books per month in a whole variety of countries across the globe. After recently re-joining the Antiquarian Booksellers Association, and with the strong family links within the trade, and a vast and growing collection of over 10,000 rare books, the Kerr family business is in good hands and has a strong future ahead.

The company has grown significantly through the online expansion, and John now works in the business with his son Robert, who joined recently after working as an auctioneer for a few years. 'Rob got involved of his own accord, no pressure from me', John states reassuringly. Like him, his younger son, Stuart, has decided to pursue another career, 'but the door is always open for him if he ever wanted to become involved', John adds respectfully.

The emergence of digital technology has meant that Kerr's Books has grown exponentially. They know and understand their trade, and realise that there is still a big market for people who want a genuine book, the first edition or an attractive reprint. They are marketing to collectors, people who value books for their history and their condition, and not necessarily just for the information their pages hold. It takes time and patience to be trained in dealing antiquarian books, the ability to recognise collectable authors, rare bindings, or first editions. A book's value is something that can only grow organically over time. Recently they have sourced a very prestigious 18th century French atlas with double page maps all hand coloured in outline. 'It is unusual to find these maps in their original form. As such they are few and far between outside of libraries' John confirms. Books of this value are becoming increasingly scarce so to find one is quite a coup for Kerr Books, and they hope to sell it for a substantial sum.

Kerr's Books and Cartmel

Cartmel is the perfect setting for an antiquarian bookshop, and not just aesthetically. The recent surge in tourism has also increased business in the shop, particularly in the summer months as people come to the village to learn about history, and where better than in an antiquarian bookshop? John is extremely pleased with his decision to move back to the village. He grew up here and feels a great sense of belonging. 'Now people are more mobile, we don't connect with place anymore and I think it is important to do so'. In some way John always knew that one day he would come back to follow in the footsteps of his predecessors, and continue the Kerr legacy into the next generation.

Lydia Crowe

-

The elegant lady in the baggy coat

Perched on a hand in a thick leather glove sits a large bird, his undistracted focus on the daily catch. His windswept owner – dressed in a warm, baggy coat, blue worn jeans, and thick leather boots – releases him as he stretches out his magnificent wings, and rises up in to the morning sun. He glides up to the nearest tree and together they start their daylight hunt. From the treetop he can feel a peculiar magnetism drawing him towards his find – the beckoning pull of his stomach. Suddenly, in the heart of this vast and open field, a rabbit is rudely startled out of its somnolent morning daze by a large swoop of air. It begins to flee, darting from left to right, when ominous wings smoothly glide overhead waiting for the best time to capture the prey. In this moment the elegant lady in the baggy coat is filled with a sense of calm and stillness as her everyday worries vanish behind enfolding fields and fells.

The hawk, Aubin, appears like a small speck in the sky as he sores high. His wings glisten in the morning sun and he majestically dances beneath the pink and orange clouds. Without warning this otherworldly scene transforms as Aubin tucks in his wings and begins to dive, his silhouette growing larger while he plummets back to earth. The young rabbit, aware of his presence, continues to dash erratically across the field seeking safety, but it is too late as in an instant large claws slam into this delectable treat. The elegant lady's eyes glisten and she cheers in excitement – a similar sound to that of a proud mother watching her child win a first medal in the school race. She rewards him with some meat from her side pouch in exchange for his daily catch.

Lydia out on the field ©Lydia Crowe

This exchange has been repeated for over 4,000 years. From ancient beginnings in Middle Eastern hills, to the prairies of America and the forests of Europe, the art of falconry is now practiced on all the continents. For generations falconers worldwide have passed along their knowledge and skills adapting and transforming this art into the 21st century.

Falconry has long been regarded as the 'sport of kings' and although it continues to be predominantly a male sport, there is a long and illustrious history of female falconers. Those of most notoriety include Mary, Queen of Scots who was allowed to fly a merlin from her window during her imprisonment; Elizabeth I who was an avid falconer; Eleanor of Aquitaine, one of the wealthiest and most powerful women in the world during the high Middle Ages; and today Ashol Pan, a 13-year-old from Mongolia, who is one of the last remaining Mongolian eagle falconers. Lydia follows in the footsteps of these regal falconers, allowing the beauty and elegance of the sport to continue to shine through her.

Today Lydia Crowe – the elegant lady in the baggy coat – continues this age-old practice in the fields and hills surrounding Cartmel.

Growing up

It is difficult not to develop an affinity for nature when you grow up absorbing so much natural beauty. The outdoors are your playground and Mother Nature is your guide. You trek through forests with your parents, play hide and seek in the trees, watch for trolls as you cross bridges and paddle in streams. As you grow in height and courage you build rafts and dens out of nearby twigs and grass, climb up trees to the highest branch and jump in lakes, all the time fearlessly forging your own special relationship with your environment. However, when the young people from the village and surrounding area graduate from the local secondary school, the memories of this connection will be just that, as they wilt like falling leaves, during their transition into adulthood. For most, the desire to seek outdoor adventures, climb trees and frolic through fields is replaced with the pursuit of a top job within a big city corporation and the entrapment of consumerism. It takes a truly unique person to be able to take this innocent and rare connection with nature into adulthood.

Lydia was raised in a small house just outside of Cartmel by her parents Paul and Audrey, who also shared her love for nature, and this had a profound influence over her upbringing. They always supported her wild pursuits and gave her a sense of freedom that perhaps would be unobtainable if she had been raised elsewhere. During her childhood she would spend hours outdoors watching birds, studying animals and immersing herself in the natural surroundings. As with any inquisitive child her interest led to action, and by nine Lydia had already transformed their shed into an asylum for lost and injured wildlife. Paul (her father) was happy to help his daughter, and they opened their doors to a variety of different species that were in need of help. Orphaned hedgehogs, birds that had lost their flight and lost dogs were all offered sanctuary, until they regained strength and returned to where they belonged. It was during this period that her love for birds began to develop, and when she turned 14 her ever-doting father built her an aviary half the size of the garden to house her newly acquired tropical finches. For her this is where it all really began.

As Lydia grew in age the outdoors began to infiltrate even farther inside. Large tubs full of soil, twigs and leaves found space on her bathroom windowsill, under the bed and on top of the kitchen fridge, housing woodlice, earthworms and stick inserts. Today, her earthworms, stick insects and small rodents have been replaced by their predators – birds of prey. Her tubs of soil and twigs have transformed into incubators containing a wealth of eggs of many different shapes and sizes. Once these rare and tiny falcons hatch and take their first breaths, their mother, Lydia, has to ensure that their demanding mouths are never empty, and that their bellies are always filled. To sate the appetite of these fast-growing chicks Lydia had to store road kill in the freezer, and defrost rats and quails on her windowsills, until she was able to move them out of the house and into their custom-made aviaries.

The transformative power of exploration

After graduating from University in 2010 with a degree in business Lydia began to pursue a more conventional career path as a recruitment consultant. Though this is a good and stable job for some, the long days of sitting inside a small office in front of a computer, endlessly keeping on top of her emails and trying to push sales almost drove her to despair. The idea of the 'rat race' seemed empty and pointless and she made the bold decision to leave after the end of the first year. Though many thought she was mad to leave the position in a time of economic austerity, Lydia listened to her heart and took the plunge.

In these times of social and environmental urgency, when calculating minds would like us to ignore anything that directly or indirectly opposes capitalism, and when nihilistic power engulfs most forms of potential activism, an alternative thinker with a curious mind is a rare thing. Most people are content and settled in the life they have built for themselves and don't have any desire to step out and question what is around them. Lydia is one of these rare people and has an unquenchable hunger to explore and progress beyond what is comfortable and familiar.

For Lydia, the feeling of waking up in new cities and immersing herself in fresh experiences and different cultures is extremely empowering, and has brought new and diverse perspectives to her life. From wild pursuits in the Sri Lankan rainforest, trekking with orangutans in Borneo, surfing the waves of Morocco and partying all night in India, Lydia has experienced a whole host of adventures on her travels. From Asia to Europe to Africa, she has stepped across a diverse spectrum of countries and cultures, each adding to her unique understanding of the world.

After leaving her job, her insatiable desire to travel again took flight, and she saved money so that she could take herself on a solo trek through the Nepalese Himalayas. She came back from the Himalayas feeling reenergized and with renewed perspective, and knew her dream was to pursue a career in falconry. She combined her skills and talents, and after four years of learning the necessary skills to become an expert in falconry, she founded her own business – Lyth Valley Falconry – set up in order to share her passion for birds and knowledge of falconry with others. Through this she aims to fly birds in natural beautiful surroundings where they feel at home and perform at their best. In her eyes there is simply nothing better than spending an afternoon on the hill with a falcon, or wandering deep into the woods on a hawking expedition.

You can now find Lydia every morning flying her birds in the local fields around Cartmel, her calm and peaceful aura emanating across the boundless fields. From now on she will forever be the elegant lady in the baggy coat who had the courage and determination to turn her dreams into her reality.

Richard English

–

The Yorkshire lad with Cumbrian charm

On a dark and misty night, the village lies silent as silhouettes of the final punters from the pubs stagger through the Square after a late night. There are no streetlights but beams from passing cars cut through the fog shining round the stone archway as they light up the path past the Cavendish Arms. The bar lady waves off her final customers then slams and bolts the heavy wooden door, and turns into the silence of the empty pub. Landlord Richard English and his wife, Donna, are in the back office sorting out the nightly finances, and the bar lady stands alone. There is something eerie about the silence following a loud and bustling evening, and after a night of serving others now the bar lady is alone with her thoughts. She steadies her inner monologue and gets back to the task at hand, taking out the mop to clean down and close up for the night. She motivates herself, thinking about how nice it will be to get home, and sit down with a warm cup of tea after a hard night's graft.

Inside this quintessentially British pub, the ambers from the old stone fire crack and whisper as they fade into the night. The wooden beams overhead creak in the silence, as the Cavendish Arms also prepares for its nightly rest. The bar lady is familiar with these haunting sounds, but is nonetheless intimidated by their presence in the quietness. She takes out the hoover in an attempt to drown out the silence, distracting herself by focusing on cleaning the patterns on the green and blue flowery carpet. Ensuring not a spot is missed she heads backwards towards the windows, when suddenly a loud bang hits the glass startling her as she spins around. Heart racing she looks at the window on the left, in the blackness she tries to adjust her eyes

Richard English

to the outside darkness but she can't see anything. Then suddenly, to the right a local punter, Jack Park, with a beaming smile on his face giggles and waves mischievously as he walks away. Relieved, she waves back laughing to herself and gets back to the task at hand.

She finishes her hoovering, unplugs the cord and walks to take it back round the bar to the cupboard. She opens the wooden door and walks inside, placing it in its usual spot by the painted white stonewall inside the cupboard. Pulling the cord, she switches the light off and walks out, slowly closing the door. As the door swings shut she notices something out of the corner of her eye that looks like the shadow of a person, her heart racing, she freezes. She has heard stories of a ghostly presence before but has never actually seen it for herself. Momentarily calming herself, she knows she must look again and using the door for support she turns to the corner of the room where a little old woman with long black hair covered by a white bonnet is sat staring at her. The two freeze in a timeless glare. This is no regular customer, and no one that she recognises; she seems to be from another time and place. Petrified, she stares until she turns pale, screams and runs to the back office to find Richard and his wife, and tells them of her paranormal encounter.

This is not the first sighting of a lady of this description. In fact there have been a few over the years. Richard himself doesn't know whether to believe it but there have been a number of inexplicable occurrences, including doors mysteriously locking by themselves, things moving spontaneously and sightings by other customers. This might not be surprising in a pub just under 500 years old, but is nonetheless frightening.

Richard, the Cavendish Arms, and his staff

The Cavendish Arms is located through the gatehouse archway just off the Square. The pub was previously a coach inn for horses and carts, and dates back 465 years. Records show that as long as the Priory Church has been there, this site has always been used as an inn, a hostel or a brewery. Downstairs the pub maintains a quaint old-style British aesthetic, with low-beamed ceilings, patterned carpets, wooden furniture and a blazing log fire, a tranquil place known for its good food and local craft ales. Upstairs in the rickety loft (a place customers no longer go) one can still see the long and rich history of the building. Layers and layers of wallpaper that were once carefully pasted on top of each other, are now all peeling away to unveil a 'wall book' that you can date back, time and time again. On the left side is an original disused cockfighting pit, a now discredited 'sport' pitting two aggressive roosters against each other. The building was located inside the village when the medieval walls were up, and according to folklore the pub was rebuilt from the ruins of the original walls. All these features make the building very unique, and give the pub a special place in the hearts of villagers.

Richard English, the current owner of the Cavendish Arms, moved to Cartmel in 2002 after a long career in hospitality. At the time he was running a Spanish tapas restaurant in Leeds, but was disillusioned and in need of a change. He visited the Lake District to find somewhere to take over, 'any place we found had to meet two criteria', Richard recalls. 'One, it had to be a place that wasn't as successful as it could be but had potential, and two, for my wife Donna, it had to be a scenic place where she could safely bring up our children. Cartmel and the Cavendish met all these requirements, so we bought the lease and took over on the 25th of November 2002, and we haven't looked back since'.

It is not an easy venture to take over a pub, and certainly not something to take lightly. Brewery rates especially in popular areas such as Cartmel, are astronomical, and have caused the collapse of countless pubs across the country for owners who were unable to meet the demands. Other pubs in the village have frequently changed hands since Richard has owned the Cavendish. According to Richard, his recipe for success is the people who work for him: 'Every pub serves good food and drinks, but what sets them apart is the people who sell it' he says. His staff are a dedicated team, many of whom worked at the pub even before he took over the lease. To Richard, this longevity is vital for the survival of a pub.

Cartmel and its characters

As we have learnt, Cartmel is bursting with charming characters, and what better place to meet them than in the pub. Even though Cartmel has changed in recent years as it becomes an increasingly popular tourist destination, pubs still provide a place where local people come together, and a place you will always see someone you know. You become a kind of family who support and care for each other, making sure the elderly are never lonely and always have someone to chat with. As a bar worker you become a friend to everyone, and a local counsellor as people drunkenly confide in you their deepest secrets, and since taking over the pub Richard has seen it all, the good, the bad and the ugly.

Of course, we were not able to cover every character in the village when writing this book, but through the eyes of the bar staff at the Cavendish Arms we hope to introduce you to a few more who have not been featured. One of Richard's most memorable customers was Ronnie Tallon. Ronnie was a regular in all the pubs across the local area, and popped into the Cavendish for his daily pint (or two). He was left unable to work at 40 after being severely beaten by a mob of young men. The attack induced a premature stroke, and he suffered from mild brain damage. Ronnie spent the rest of his life wandering around all the local pubs, umbrella in hand and dressed in a brown cotton coat. After many years of alcoholism, at 60 he was warned by the doctor to stop drinking pints, but in keeping with his comical view on life he continued to drink the same amount but in half pints. He became a regular and well-loved customer in the Cavendish Arms and came in for regular chats with Richard, staff and other visiting customers. He would regularly recount about the young lads that beat him and left him for dead, the moment that changed his life forever. He talked of his estranged twin brother Donald, his ex-wife Susan, his dog he called Susan, and would quip in an overly posh accent that 'the dog was much better behaved than the wife, darling'. He would finish each sentence and rude comment with, 'I know, I know', or 'oh, I am naughty, aren't I darling' sometimes reaching to tickle the listener under the chin with his long nails. He was a much-loved character in the village, but sadly Ronnie passed away in 2013, the after-effects of his former attack having caught up with him.

Another infamous customer, now known as 'the unidentified man', entered the village in 2007 pulling up in his old style Rolls Royce and went by the name of Anthony De Klerk. He was a very tall man, who wore brown tweed jackets, matching trousers, cleanly pressed white shirts and thin-framed glasses that sat at the end of his nose. He was a charmer and spoke with a deep Belgian accent as he told stories of being a descendent of Belgian nobility, a member of the House of Lords, a chef and a businessman, amongst many other guises. His charismatic and suave demeanour seduced the villagers as he flashed his wallet full of fifty-pound notes, bought champagne and bottles of top-shelf whiskey. A brilliant musician, he played the cornet and a variety of other instruments on his visits to the local pubs. In the end it emerged that he was a very sophisticated conman who had been sweet-talking businesses and families out of thousands of pounds. When living near Cartmel, he was appointed the manager of the Graythwaite Manor in Grange-over-Sands. He started out as a chef, and wormed his way in becoming close friends with the owners. As he became aware that they were having trouble with the business, he offered to help to manage the hotel. Taken in by his charm the owners gave him the job, which meant that he had access to their bank accounts. This proved to be a catastrophic mistake as he spent £100,000 of their money, boasting of his wealth, whilst he bankrupted the business. He was caught in 2008 and spent two and a half years in prison for deception and fraud. To this day neither the police nor the locals know his real name.

Many celebrities also frequent the village, and one who has visited the Cavendish Arms on numerous occasions is Sir Ian McKellen. He was a great person to have around the village and you would often see him dressed casually in blue jeans and a white vest top. His down-to-earth presence meant that he wasn't harassed and was just left to go about his business as if he was a local. Another celebrity who would visit the pub occasionally is Richard's wife's relative who played football for England when they won the World Cup in 1966. Every four years when the World Cup is on he becomes famous again, and his phone rings with press trying to get quotes about what it felt like to win. He escapes this onslaught by discretely coming to the Cavendish Arms. He sits quietly in the corner of the pub watching the matches from afar, unbeknownst to the customers that they are sitting with one of England's great footballers. Not to blow his cover and disturb his peace, I won't reveal his name here.

Richard himself is a key character from the village, and has succeeded in helping the Cavendish Arms to evolve and keep up with the times, whilst also maintaining its rustic charm and old soul. The pub is a central hub in the village. It's quirky, quaint and quiet and is the perfect place to sample local ales, eat some good pub food, and of course meet and chat to village characters.

Steve Chamberlain

—

Chief proprietor of Chamberlains' Gift Emporium

'We started off about eleven years ago, and since then we have evolved into a really successful gift shop. Trade is excellent, mainly due to L'Enclume. We try and have an eclectic mix of things in, we like to stock things that you can't get anywhere else. A lot of the stuff we buy is actually off stage and film sets, my nephew is in television. We also sell a lot of products made locally, for example, the dresses are made by a girl in Allithwaite, the woodworks by a man that lives in Field Broughton. So we try to support as many local produces as we can.

One of my biggest sellers is the full-sized sheep and cows, we sell an awful lot of those, we are even nicknamed 'The Sheep Shop'. In fact, there was a lady that came in, she was from Southampton, and she wanted two sheep for her husband and a lamb. I told her that we can't deliver them because they cost too much, but I told her that my nephew lives in London so if she could meet me at London Gateway I could drop them off. So we arranged it, and then at the last minute she realised that the drop off day was on her husband's 70th birthday. So I said my nephew lives in Muswell Hill, so she went to pick them up from there. The next day I got a parcel from Amazon containing a bottle of brandy and a thank you card from the lady, and a request to continue selling the sheep to her. So now every other month I take ten sheep down and meet her at London Gateway to drop them off. I take them down in the back of a van and she collects them in a horsebox. So that is just one example of the unusual things that happen in this shop'.

Steve Chamberlain

Dr Richard Fell

-

The man with a thousand and one stories

The rattling of trolley wheels echoes gently through the busy hum of the hospital ward, as the two orderlies make their way through the fast-paced bustle towards the light at the end of the double doors. Nurses dressed in white aprons and large white hats sombrely glance back as the trolley passes, momentarily engrossed in sadness before switching back to the task at hand. The patient in question was female, a new mother, who, unable to cope with the thought of rearing an unwanted child had taken her own life. As the trolley continues past each doorway the light flicks over the patient, as if it were casting the last wave of goodbye on her way out. The gurney glides past the last doorway and as the final ray of light casts its shadow a quick sighting from Dr Fell, who catches a glance at the hand of this female patient, prompts him to shout, 'Wait a minute!' as he ran towards the bed, 'she's not ready to go yet – she is still alive!'. Although the rest of her body was a deathly pallor and her body temperature was down to $18°C$, her nails had specks of pink on them, which meant that there was still some oxygen in her blood and therefore a chance to save her.

This was the first time anything like this had been attempted, and Dr Fell and his colleague, Dr John Lloyd, and their team frantically fought to save the woman's life. That afternoon they worked together to insert the necessary tubes and performed cardiopulmonary bypass that immediately revived the patient as soon as the blood hit the brain. From this day on Dr Richard Fell and his team have held the record for the coldest person ever resuscitated. 'This is not the first time this has happened', Richard explained as we sit drinking a beer in the Royal Oak Bar in Carmel. 'It is not

Richard Fell and his dog Jeep

uncommon for people to wake up in a mortuary, after being presumed dead'. 'What happened to the lady?' I ask. 'Well, the first constructive thing she did after she recovered was sit up in bed as a nurse offered her a cup of tea, and she took the cup and threw it all over the nurse. I think she was devastated that her suicide attempt had failed, and she was again faced with the reality of having a now two-week-old child'.

Richard has had a long and prolific career working as a doctor and specialising in anaesthetics and intensive care for over 40 years. He began in 1962 in Poole General Hospital, and moved around various hospitals in the South of England during the course of his career. His fascination with anaesthetics came after he read the research of the famous Dr Spencer Wells, who described the first surgical procedure performed using general anaesthetics that caused deep vein thrombosis followed by a clot on the lung. It was because of this finding that he advocated local anaesthetics as much as possible, as a safer alternative. During his long and illustrious career he worked as a lecturer at the University of Oxford, and later worked in hospitals in Slough and Windsor, where he was on call for the Royal family. Although he showed the Queen around one of the hospitals he worked in, the only time he was called on duty to attend to a member of the Royal family was when Prince Charles's face was hit by a horse's hoof in a polo accident, but Charles refused any anaesthetic, as he feared the consequences. So Richard was no longer needed, and true to his character he hung up his white coat and headed to the pub. Some other of Richard's regular patients were the infamous Kray brothers, who together wreaked havoc on the streets of London in the 1950s and 1960s until they were caught and institutionalized. Richard treated them for a variety of different injuries, and he also treated those who had been kneecapped by them. In return he was always offered a free pint or two when he popped down to the Kray brothers' pub.

If you catch up with Dr Richard Fell for his daily pints of local ale in Cartmel you will discover all manner of interesting stories and anecdotes, like the ones above. Tales of triumph and tragedy, comedy and history. He will tell stories from his long ancestry of pioneering explorers, and his own illustrious life, some of which I will share with you now.

Tales through time

This story begins just over 400 years ago with a family of shepherds who resided in a small coastal village in the south of Cumbria. Surrounded by vast fields and lush green forests, they were humble people who lived and worked on the land. England was under the rule of Henry VIII, and the Tudor period was in full swing, the country at this time was sparsely populated and efforts to expand cities had just begun, so most people worked as subsistence farmers. It was a time of change and growth, but most people, like the Fell family, had to work hard and struggled to survive. At this time the Fells made their living tending to the cattle belonging to the Penningtons of Muncaster Castle. The Penningtons came from a powerful lineage, and were not people to be messed with. Ascent through the class system was difficult during this time, and for over 200 years the Fells worked in these fields, tending to the cattle and watching over the Penningtons' wealth. Frustrated with his lowly lot, a later descendent of Mr Fell stole sheep from the Pennington family and this led to his conviction in a Leeds court. Fortunately for him the death penalty had just been withdrawn for sheep steeling, so his life was spared.

    Listening to this story one is left with many questions: to which community did the Fell family feel they belonged? What happened to the imprisoned Fell? What was it like to live in a village in England in the 1600s? One thing is for sure, the Fells were destined for more prosperous futures than shepherding, and this is proven in what was to come.

The rise of the Fells

Back with our pint of beer, Richard lets out a loud chuckle, 'You know, one of the children of the Fells during the 1600s married the daughter of the postmaster, and from then on every single generation has passed on double the amount of money than the one before!'. He pauses for a second and jovially continues, 'That is, until now, now we are on the way down'.

    Despite growing up in India and the South of England after the war, Richard had always had a deep connection with the Lake District. In a story reminiscent of the aristocratic 1600s, Richard's great-grandfather worked as an agent to Lord and Lady Cavendish of Holker, a neighbouring village to Cartmel. Great-grandfather Fell of the 1800s would look after the daily affairs of the Cavendish family, and was responsible for selling the land acquired for the Carnforth to Barrow railway line, which is still in use today. His great-grandfather had fourteen children, all of whom became pioneering and highly influential people in their own right. Two of the siblings became knights, including Richard's own grandfather Sir Bryan; another sibling married the famous hymn composer John Bacchus Dykes; others built mansions in the United States; and some married into great fortunes. Some of my favourite anecdotes of these fourteen siblings are taken from two specific periods in time, and are stories of discovery and exploration.

Sometime in 1899 in Arnside, Cumbria: A young boy holding a flickering candlelight makes his way up the narrow creaking staircase, down the dimly lit hall. Walking slowly, with slight hesitation, he continues down the hallway until he arrives at the third door on the left of the hall. He pauses and slowly pushes the door. It makes a creaking sound as it opens. As he makes his way through the door and into the room, his candle casts light onto a wooden dressing table with a dusty mirror on top, as he looks into the glass he sees the room reflected back at him. He's where he needs to be. Making his way over to the side of the bed, he kneels down and reaches for the hand of the sleeping man. Reverend James Fell, who was vicar of Arnside at the time, turns and calmly looks down at the young boy, who softly utters, 'please come to San Francisco Sir, we need your help'. The boy repeated this two or three times, until he faded back into the night. James Fell suddenly awoke, and realized that the vision or dream he had just experienced must have meant something. This was his calling. So he sent an urgent request to the Bishop of Carlisle to care for his family while he was away, he had had his calling and he was going to San Francisco. James packed his bags and arrived in San Francisco later in 1899, and it was here that he founded the Mission to Seamen that is still running to this day. If you travel to San Francisco, you can find a street named after James Fell (Fell Street), which Richard went to visit in 1992.

Sometime in 1908 in Victorian England: A horse and carriage clatters over the cobbles on a cold and frosty morning on Harley Street, London. Men with tall hats and black suits make their way along the street, all of them doctors or medical professionals of some kind. Among them is another of the fourteen Fell children, a radiologist, and a pioneer in his own right as he works to supply the first x-ray services to the people of London.

His patients include some of London's most affluent residents, and he is well-known for his new-found technology and skills. Harley Street was the place of professionals, and one had to exude maturity in order to inspire confidence in clients. Unfortunately for Dr Fell, despite being qualified as a doctor, he had maintained Dorian Gray looks. Therefore, in order to seem professional he paid one of his fellow medical students, who had gone prematurely bald, to sit in the window of his surgery so that people didn't feel like they were going to be treated by an adolescent. Despite his long and transformative career in advancing medical technology, the effects of performing x-rays were unknown at the time, and Dr Fell later tragically died of leukemia.

All roots lead to Cartmel

In 2006 Richard retired from working in Windsor and came to make a new home in the Lake District. As I mentioned, it is a place of deep ancestral significance for him, and after a catastrophic marriage he felt he needed to come back to a place to which he felt connected. Throughout his family history he had always been aware of the Cartmel Peninsula, and had always intended on retiring there. After finding a home for sale on the corner of the road he and his father used to take when visiting his grandfather, he felt that it was serendipitous, and he bought it straight away. He got his dog and loyal companion Jeep in 2007, and the pair has been inseparable since.

Since moving here Richard has become an integral part of the local community. He is a kind-hearted, polite gentleman who always has an interesting story to tell, or wise advice to give. If you visit Cartmel you can find Richard and Jeep in almost every pub at some point each week. Once you find him be sure to buy him a pint of local ale, and maybe, if you're lucky he might even tell you a story.

Tiffany Hunt

-

The lady with a legacy

The kettle whistles on top of the stove, and Tiffany rushes over to take it off, pulling a red and white checked towel to protect her hands on her way. She pours us both coffee and we sit around the large wooden table in the middle of her kitchen. As I glance to my right I am struck by the perfect positioning of her home, there standing in all its glory is the east facing side of the Priory Church, large windows glistening in the sun. To the left is her beautiful garden, filled with the first buds of spring. Her cat purrs and rubs against my leg and I tickle its chin, as I position myself on the floral cushion ensuring it masks the hard wooden chair.

Low wooden beams hang overhead and dark grey stone floors below give added ambience to this 18th century home. As we finish our coffee Tiffany gives me the guided tour around the hall, kitchen and living room. She shows me an array of abstract paintings by her mother who was an artist, an old map of the peninsula and a variety of pictures, each one telling a different story and history.

It's a Sunday morning and her house is bustling. Her sister Annabel comes in and speedily makes her way around the kitchen as she boils soup for their visiting cousin. I am already their third visitor for the day and a stream of people are still making their way through the door. Some drop off books, others just pop in for a quick chat, but with each passing person I can see that the Hunt sisters are very much part of the community of Cartmel.

Tiffany and Annabel have been living together for three years now, and when Tiffany bought the house, it was the first time it had been on the market since 1960. Coincidentally the previous owners were also siblings,

Tiffany Hunt

two brothers, Rev'd John Dickinson and Bernard Dickinson who lived together for many years. The brothers were the complete opposite from one another. John was academic and wrote a book entitled *The Land of Cartmel*, documenting the history of the village and had just retired from working as a professor at the University of Birmingham. His brother Bernard, however, was more practical. They came from a long line of racehorse trainers, so were keen horseracing enthusiasts, and fitted the village perfectly. Sadly, they were involved in a car accident on a dangerous turn not so far from Cartmel and John died as a result. He had left the house to Bernard, who lived alone there for a few more years. When he passed away, he left the house to a convent so they could use it as a retreat. It was barely used for a number of years, and came on the market once they decided to sell. Tiffany knew John and Bernard well. John was one of the first people her parents met when they arrived in the village. 'This was one of the first things we discovered about Cartmel', Tiffany explains. 'It's a very small world. Wherever you come from you are going to find a connection with things'.

Rediscovered Cartmel heritage

Although she had visited or passed through a few times, Tiffany's first visit to Cartmel was in 1981. One of her oldest childhood friends had just moved to the area and had made Tiffany godmother to her daughter, who was being christened in the Priory Church. It was here that she first stepped upon what would later become her street. On the recommendation of her friend she went to look at a property that would soon become her parents' retirement home.

A career woman, Tiffany visited Cartmel and her parents over next two decades, and during that time her connections with the place deepened. Although they moved into the village as outsiders, the family soon discovered that their heritage stretched back. As they started researching into their family history they found records that showed that their forebears had lived in Cartmel and married in the Priory in around 1799. This rediscovered connection made everything fall into place. In 2002 Tiffany came back to work in North West England and felt the need to be closer to her family, so decided to buy the property both she and her sister live in today, which was then two doors down from her parents' house.

A few years later her mother fell ill with dementia, and since her father had passed away in 1994, it was up to Tiffany and Annabel to care for her. Annabel quit her job in London and moved in with her mother to become her carer, and later Tiffany retired and they both looked after her for around eight years until she died. The sisters then decided to sell their mother's house and moved into Tiffany's, which is where they live now.

They have lived together for three years, and have never regretted their decision. Both take a very active role in village life: Tiffany was the chair of Cartmel in Bloom and Cartmel Village Society for a few years before handing it over to David and Linda Crabtree. Annabel works a lot with the Priory Church, she is Rev'd Nick Devenish's personal assistant, and Tiffany is also on the Priory's Parochial Church Council.

A career in preserving heritage

Tiffany grew up in Preston in Lancashire. Her father was a doctor and her mother was a trained artist. She was brought up in an environment with endless opportunities and was told that she could be anything she wanted to be – something that would stand her in good stead for her future career path. Her mother was keen to build an appreciation for art and history, and on days when it was too wet to go for a walk she would plan an outing to a church, an old building or an art exhibition. As children, Tiffany and her sister found this incredibly boring, but these experiences had a profound influence and later grew into passions.

Tiffany grew up in the 1950s and 60s, a time when Britain was still an industrial hub. Preston was a strong cotton-manufacturing town, with flourishing docks. 'My father's practice was in inner-city Preston and I can still remember the sign on the front of a large mill we went past on our way to school, which said, "Horrocks, the greatest name in cotton", she recalls. Of course, much has changed now. Many of Britain's once-thriving manufacturing industries have declined and in many places only the shells of empty mill buildings remain. Looking at how to find sustainable uses for some of these disused industrial buildings in the North West and Yorkshire were just one of the aspects of Tiffany's work during her 28 year career working for the National Trust and latterly in her current role as Chair of the North West Committee of the Heritage Lottery Fund.

Tiffany started working for The National Trust in 1982 and has fulfilled a number of different roles within the organisation, becoming the Trust's first female Regional Director in Northumbria in 1992. 'This was so novel at that time that I featured on Women's Hour, and was profiled in *Country Life Magazine*. It just shows how the role of women has changed, as now you can find many more women in senior positions', she reflects. Despite the pressures of a demanding job, she thoroughly enjoyed her time as a Regional Director in Northumbria and Yorkshire, before her last job as Director of the North West.

'There were no two days the same' she explains. 'In a day I could be out and about talking to one of our hill farming tenants in the morning followed by meetings with colleagues or external connections rounding off the day with a speaking engagement. It really was such a privilege'. Tiffany worked on a huge variety of projects during her time with the National Trust encompassing historic buildings, countryside and coastal properties. One such was opening the childhood home of John Lennon in Liverpool. Memorably she helped host Yoko Ono at the opening. 'I'll never forget it. We were in a semi-detached house with a marquee at the back with a large press corps squeezed inside. Because of Yoko Ono's presence some of the neighbouring roads had to be closed for her arrival, but despite the disruption, there were no complaints, we were just so proud and pleased', Tiffany adds.

At one point every year she would work as a volunteer for the day to see how everything worked. One year she chose to work at the Beatrix Potter's Hill Top talking to visitors and volunteers. Children were greeted at the door of the house and presented with the loan of a book, so that they could match the illustrations to the house. 'I was particularly interested in the children's viewpoints, they see things so differently to adult eyes' Tiffany explains, 'I remember this one little boy, he must have only been around seven. He was very serious and when I asked him to tell me what he thought he said he thought it was good, but couldn't find the rat in the skirting board'. From that moment on the Trust made sure that there was, in the Potter house, a special place for children to discover the rat hole in the skirting board.

Tiffany has a passion for discovering and protecting heritage, and for bringing tangible benefits to communities across the UK. She helps to bring people together, forging partnerships and connections so that people can work together to protect Britain's heritage. In 2014 she was awarded an

MBE for her services to heritage in the North West.

Heritage in Cartmel

Now Tiffany has found a place in the historical village of Cartmel, which seems like the perfect location for someone with her interests. From the Priory, to the school, to the houses located across the village, the walls of Cartmel are filled with rich heritage that can be traced back for centuries. The National Trust owns one building in the village, the Cartmel Priory Gatehouse, which was built in around 1330-1340 in response to a Scottish raid, and acted as a deterrent to groups thinking about attacking the Priory. Following the Dissolution of the Monasteries in the 1530s the Gatehouse was saved along with the Priory Church. It has served many purposes since that time, including as a grammar school from 1624 to 1790. Then it became a museum in 1923 and was bought by the National Trust in 1946.

Despite arriving in the village later in life Tiffany feels very much part of the community in Cartmel. When her mother was ill neighbours were incredibly supportive and kind, and being part of groups like the Cartmel Village Society and Cartmel Choral Society has meant that she feels a strong sense of belonging here. She feels very strongly about the village's conservation, and has used her skills and experience to help ensure that its heritage is maintained. She was, for example, involved in raising over £200,000 locally for repairs to the Priory and the restoration of the organ. 'I don't think something should be protected so that it never changes, but where change happens, it should enhance not detract from the village's heritage' she says. 'There is something special about Cartmel. The National Trust would describe it as "spirit of place" - a tangible and intangible essence that needs to be valued so that its legacies can be enjoyed by future generations'.

Lord Hugh Cavendish

-

The green-fingered Lord

A metallic thud echoes through the ground as a trowel pushes through rocks and dirt on its way down. In a swift motion it pulls up earth, making space for the new bulbs, as they prepare to make their journey to full bloom. The cold air sends shivers through the bushes and down the back of the gardener - Lord Hugh Cavendish - as he pulls up the collar on his green-waxed jacket to avoid the chill. Although he is cold, he continues to throw handfuls of bulbs into the air, each falls into place and will come to fruition when the sun returns. Happy with his work he slowly pulls himself up, legs stiff from being on the cold ground after tending to his horticultural duties.

During winter the garden is suspended in time, waiting for the warm breeze of spring to reinvigorate it. The paths are dusted in a light layer of frost, which elegantly dances in the sun, adding sparkle to the dull light. But this serenity is broken by heavy boots crunching through the garden after a hard day's work. These footsteps startle a deer that flees into the woods. On his way up the garden Lord Cavendish passes stone griffins adorned with feather wings, a large, white wooden dovecote with multiple entrances, and The Sunken Garden - a stonewalled suntrap for anyone wanting to take a break. At the end of the path he reunites with his large gardening team, and stands chatting brushing his hand along the pruned hedgerows which provide the only colour in an otherwise grey-washed garden.

Later in the year, bees buzz, busily providing a natural eco-system as the garden begins to burst with colour when spring arrives. Lord Cavendish reappears, this time in jeans and a checked shirt. He is welcomed by an array of beautiful scents as his hard work pays off in a spectacle of colours.

Lord Cavendish at Holker Garden Festival ©Lord Hugh Cavendish

Wildflowers, pink and white lilies, blue camassias, white magnolias with a touch of yellow, are all immersed in the hues of green neat garden hedgerows and looming trees. This sight will not be wasted; it's the main exhibit at Holker Hall and seen by over 70,000 visitors per year.

Every June the family hosts the annual Holker Festival, and the stillness of winter is officially broken as thousands of families come to visit the garden. The locals showcase their best vegetables and flowers, each one bidding for the first prize. Sipping Pimms and enjoying a delicious hog roast, gardening enthusiasts explore the vast 25-acre gardens and learn about the latest gardening techniques from experts. Children and families enjoy playing, eating picnics, and sliding around the helter-skelter, while food connoisseurs sample flavours from local and UK producers.

The ever-enduring garden

Holker (pronounced "hooker" by the family) has only ever been owned by three families: the Prestons, the Lowthers of Marske and the Cavendishes, and each has influenced the gardens and house adorning it with ornaments, decorations and plants of their times. Over the last few decades Lord Hugh Cavendish, his wife Grania Cavendish and a team of gardeners have worked tirelessly to ensure that the garden is well kept and preserved, putting their own stamp on things.

Lord Cavendish traces his side of the family back to Lord George Augustus Cavendish, one of his most inspiring ancestors who lived in Holker from 1750 to 1794. Like Lord Cavendish, he was also a gardening enthusiast and introduced many new trees and plants, some of which can still be seen in the Holker Gardens today. The most prominent is the Cedar of Lebanon (Cedrus Libani), a tree that looks like it could be inspired by the African savannah with its wide flat tops and height. The illustrious history of the gardens has also been influenced by the female inhabitants of the 19th and 20th centuries. 'They are, in date order, Evelyn, the 9th Duke of Devonshire, Lady Moyra Cavendish, my grandmother and Pamela Cavendish, my mother', Lord Cavendish explains in his book *A Time to Plant*. Amongst others, these women put their mark on the gardens, planting bulbs and building the foundations for those to come. All this history puts the garden at the epicentre of the Holker family, and caring for it and opening it up for the community to enjoy epitomises the collective spirit of the Cavendish family.

With their prestigious title comes responsibility, and the family are required to be public figures centrally involved in politics and the church, both locally and nationally. Thrust into a realm of public leadership they have to ensure that their landed estates survive through sensible management and good relations with the community. 'While we make mistakes, it is clearly understood that in order to survive and prosper, we need to carry the local community with us. Our mission statement includes the requirement to have, in all our actions, regard for local people and our environment', Lord Cavendish tells me.

The Cavendishes and Cartmel

The Cavendish family have a long history in the village of Cartmel. Their estate was owned by the Priory Church until it was bought for the first and only time in 1536 following the dissolution of the monasteries. It has never been sold since, and has only changed hands through inheritance, and through the female line.

The Cartmel Racecourse has always been on land owned by the Holker Estate and the Cavendish family. The family became more active in 1974 when Lord Cavendish, an avid horseracing fan, became a director. In 1998 he bought out the previous management and since then his involvement has continued to take root. 'I minded very much having to absent myself twice in over 40 years', Lord Cavendish states during our interview. 'I have always understood the good fortune we have in the atmosphere at Cartmel Racecourse and how easily it could be lost. We need to remember always that a large number of players in National Hunt Racing make a considerable sacrifice to keep it going', he adds.

The family have always played a central role in the community, and are a neighbour and a friend to all. They have seen the changes in Cartmel over the years and in Lord Cavendish's opinion this has been extremely beneficial to the village. 'The real change came much earlier when the old inhabitants and the new arrivals learned to live with and benefit from each other. It is, I would judge, a much happier community than when I was a boy', Lord Cavendish suggests.

Lord of the manor

Lord Hugh Cavendish was born in 1941 in Holker Hall and grew up within an upper-class lifestyle, filled with privilege and opportunity. As a child he felt free as he explored the vast Holker Estate, and it was here that he unknowingly developed his love for the natural world. He was born in the middle of the World War II, the effects of which were felt within the Holker Estate, lots of their family members came to live with them and there were few staff and no gardeners. For occasional escape his parents continued to throw dinners for a wide variety of distinguished guests, including politicians and leaders from across the world, further rooting their noble standing.

But a life like this comes with certain expectations, and Lord Cavendish experienced the burdens associated with this throughout his youth. The first pressures to achieve came at school, but not just any old school; Lord Cavendish received his education at Eton College, one of the most prestigious schools in the country. He was sent away to boarding school at a young age, and always longed to be back in the Holker grounds away from the hustle of city life. There are some people who flourish in formal education and others who find it too confining, the systematic routine of achievement leaving little room for creativity. Lord Cavendish fell into the latter category and many people thought that his low attainment was a waste after so much had been invested into his education. However, Lord Cavendish discovered his calling in later life.

After leaving school at 18 with low grades, Lord Cavendish's father asked his friend, Lord Lonsdale, to give Lord Cavendish a job in the Lowther forestry department. At first working outside and undertaking manual labour in the cold was a shock for him, but after a few days on the job he discovered a camaraderie with fellow workers he had never experienced before and a love for working in nature. He therefore decided that he wanted to focus his career on working to protect the environment, but that was to be put on hold for a while.

After a few years at the forestry department he branched out to develop new skills, and moved to London to pursue a career with a merchant adventurers company. He worked for them for 10 years and spent his time living the London high life and travelling all across the world, from the Middle East, Latin America, India, Japan and to Australia, searching for business and investment opportunities for the company.

In his late twenties he was uprooted from London following the sudden death of his father. His death shook the family and left them in a state of confusion. His mother abdicated her responsibilities and suddenly Lord Cavendish found himself at the head of Holker. This new position came as quite a shock, as throughout his life Lord Cavendish felt undervalued and unappreciated. His mother didn't think that he was a worthy successor to the Holker Estate and often stated that his brother would be the one to inherit their fortunes, so he never felt like he would take over. But the position came as a welcome change. The London life came at a price, the stress combined with an intense social life meant that Lord Cavendish had developed a drinking problem during his time there. This change gave him a new perspective and finally made him confront his long-standing problem with alcohol. His experiences in London had also prepared him for managing the Holker Estate. He came back with a savvy eye for business and a vision for what was necessary to continue develop Holker Estate, a place where he could finally fully realise his potential.

For 43 years Lord Cavendish devoted his life to both developing the Estate and taking part in various aspects of public life, both local and national. In order to survive, agricultural estates such as Lord Cavendish's need to significantly extend their portfolio of business. Most estates own a collection of land and houses, and although this generates a large amount of profit, it is not enough to sustain the estates. His father recognised this and invested into a building company in Barrow and a number of caravan parks, and this is something Lord Cavendish has continued. 'My rule in life is that all enterprises need to change and evolve and they all require investment. I follow the man who said "One has to change in order to stay the same"'.

Lord and Lady Cavendish married in 1970, just before they took over the Estate, and have shared the journey of enterprise, entrepreneurialism, and gardening. Together they have made a formidable team, as Holker is now one of the biggest employers in the area, providing jobs to many people in the area. With a slate business, estate gardens, a wide range of property and numerous other businesses the Holker group has changed and grown under their ownership, ensuring it is able to survive and prosper. Now the baton has been passed on to its heir and successor, their daughter – Lady Lucy Cavendish, who will continue the legacy of the Holker Estate ensuring that the community ties to Cartmel and the local area are maintained and that the gardens continue to flourish.

Cartmel Priory Church

A view over Cartmel

Beth Conroy

-

The diary of a party girl

As the alarm rings, blonde hair matted with hairspray peels off from the pillow as the young party girl rolls over to bash the alarm into silence. It is 11am and the room looks like a mini tornado has rushed through, leaving mayhem in its wake. But there is nothing natural about this disaster, make-up and clothes lay sprawled out all over the floor and on top of her bed, haphazardly parted by empty and half empty bottles of spirits and Coca-Cola, all lightly dusted in glitter giving it a magical sheen. This is a sign of a good night, or at least a very good pre-party bonanza. As the young party girl awakes from her deep, alcohol-addled slumber she lifts her weary head and prises her eyes apart battling against last night's make-up. This is a typical Sunday morning for Beth Conroy who, in her own words, 'lives to love, laugh and party'.

A horn honks outside and Beth pulls her curtains back and sees her friend's car there, waiting to take her for her morning smoke. Her grogginess is short-lived as she knocks back an energy drink and transforms back into her ever-chirpy, cheerful self. Beth is an extremely loyal and protective friend, and is well-loved by those around her. She has an inner sense of calm and a strong sense of who she is. She does not judge people based on any kind of misguided merit and extends scrupulous fairness to all around her. A loud, extroverted, confident young woman, she is the type of person who is unafraid of the potential repercussions of free expression, and is not afraid to tell you what she thinks. This gives her an air of genuine sincerity that is often lost as people try to conform to what they think is the 'right thing' to do or say. She is a whirlwind of bohemian misadventure, and

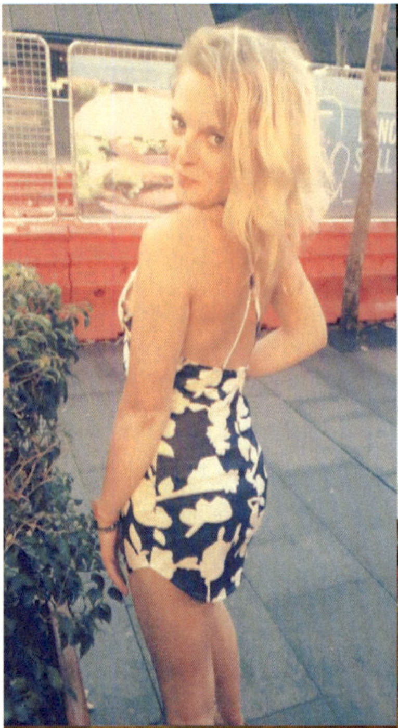
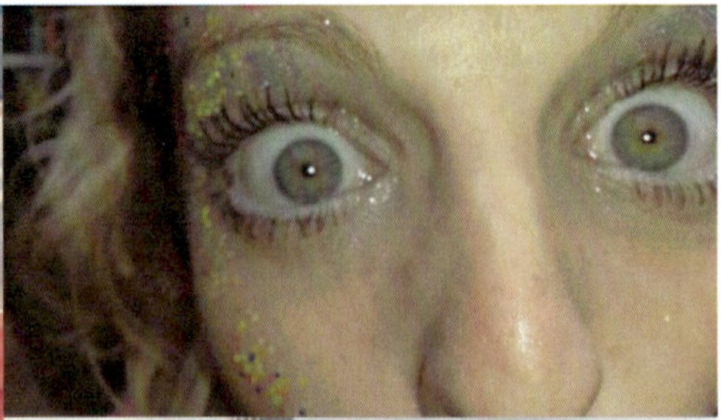
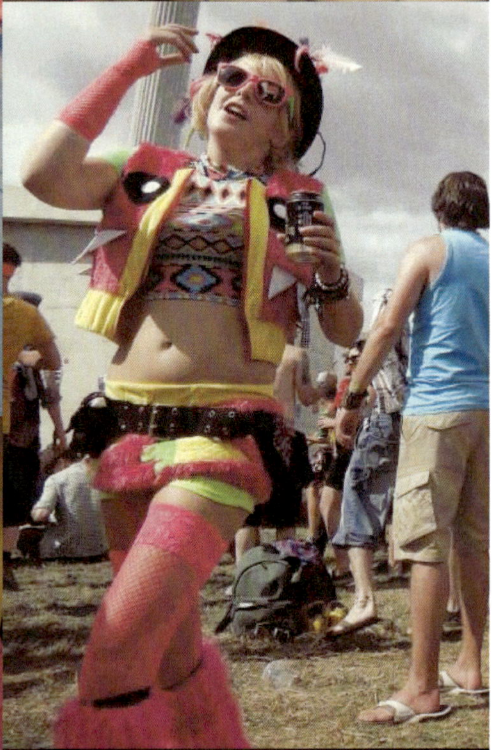
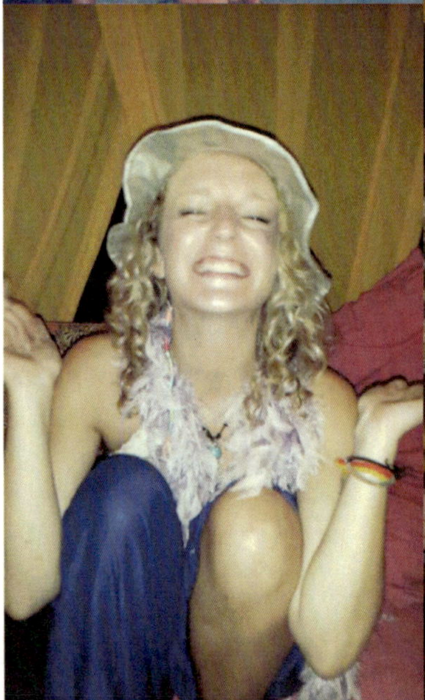
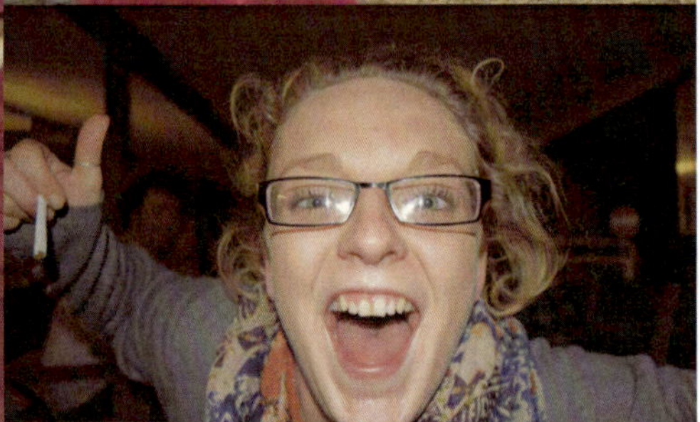

unapologetically embraces life with a vigour that might occasionally border on the reckless, but is balanced out by her child-like charm and wonder.

Saturday: The night before...

Dressed in glitter pants, a glitter crop-top and glitter covering her eyes and face, Beth hits the road with friends for a one-off festival style party – 'The Big Kids Swing'. The name says it all, and the party is for those who want to feel the freedom of their youth one last time. The party venue, The Winter Gardens in Morecambe, is a listed building. It first opened in 1897 and was of the last great seaside pleasure-palaces of the Victorian era. Inside the building retains its charm and with stained glass panels, large wooden doors, marble floors and painted murals, a different era of decadence makes this the perfect setting for a party.

The theatre echoes with sounds of electro swing, ghetto funk and vintage music, as a mix of circus acts, including a burlesque performance, pole dancing, hoop spinning and fire breathers take to the stage. It is compulsory for guests to wear their most outrageous gear, and the place is awash with clothes that look like they have been picked out from a child's dressing up box. Of course no 'big kids' party would be complete without a bouncy castle, a ball pool, and smoke machine cannons.

This is nothing out of the ordinary for Beth: raves, festivals, quirky parties, clubbing, Beth has experienced it all, in style. The fearlessness of her personality shines through in her party fashion, and her wardrobe is filled with an oft-gaudy, dizzying convergence of styles. Glitter pants, luminous skirts and tops, ballerina tutu skirts, coloured bras, funky cardigans, crop tops – these expressions of freedom hang next to the Sunday comfort clothes – tracksuit pants, jeans, wellies and jumpers.

A girl of her time

As with any period of English history, the 21st century has its own party scene, although this era is known for being more lavish and decadent than it was in the past, marked by excessive drinking, all-night parties and impolite youth. It's not all bad though, the proliferation of festival culture, night clubs and exciting and unique parties provided space for unconstrained expression and has meant that 'growing up' in many Western countries has been significantly extended, as people party well on in to their 20s and even 30s.

Whether it is in a city, town or village, each party scene affords its attendees a place of escapism and fun. In and around Cartmel there are a great number of raves, parties and social gatherings. The youth of the area are often looking to escape from what can sometimes be a boring and mundane place to grow up in, and find their release and excitement through a night out.

Cartmel is well-known for its local pubs, where you can go on any given night and always find someone you know to talk to. Over the weekends this turns into a reunion of old school friends, work colleagues and locals. There is also a covert rave scene in and around the area, which is less famous. These raves usually take place in a field in an unknown location, and its precise location is spread by word of mouth and text messages on the night. Local DJs perform and the place is decked out with lights and understated decoration. These are all scenes in which Beth plays her part.

Monday: back at work

Beth has worked in various places in the village including the Royal Oak and Cartmel Village Shop, where she was well-loved. As she walks into the village over the stream, past the shops, through the square, every person she meets, the dog walkers, early morning beer drinkers, gardeners, children heading to school, or business owners opening up for the day ahead, young or old, everyone knows Beth and each person greets her with a smile and an enthusiastic wave. She has gotten to know most people in the village either through school, working in the local pubs, working in Cartmel Village Shop or attending parties. Everyone loves her; her cheeriness, openness and reassuring confidence make people warm to her in an instant.

Though it wasn't always that way, between the ages of 13 and 16 Beth went through something that many experience in their youth – the high school rebellion.

Sometime in 2010

As the school bell rang, signalling the end of break, Beth stubbed out her cigarette, slung her bag over one shoulder and slowly made her way to class. A loud-mouthed youth she left terror in her wake as she walked down the corridors. In class she swung back on her chair, chewing gum and barely listening to the late morning teachings. When questioned about her behaviour, she would answer back, giving the teacher some witty and cheeky response. It was during this period of experimentation and of pushing the boundaries that she started going out to local parties and raves, and these proved to be the formative years for Beth.

Back to now

Of course people grow and change when leaving high school and Beth has done just that. A pioneer in her own way, she forges her own path and makes no excuses or apologies to those who judge her lifestyle. Beth embodies the kind of honesty most of us could use a little more of, giving uncensored but necessary truths, and living life the way she believes is best. She will continue to go through life in her own flamboyant, haphazard manner making the rules as she goes along. Most importantly she will have fun while she is doing it, and her sparkling personality will always shine through whether she is dressed in glitter from head to toe or wearing a jumper and wellies.

Jimmy Forbes

Jimmy enjoying a pint outside The Kings Arms

Mike

-

A.K.A Post Office Mike

'This is the village of the damned! You could write a book about life in Cartmel, anything else I say here you won't be able to use'.

Mike used to run the shop and his wife used to run the Post Office in what is now the Cartmel Village Shop.

Linda and David Crabtree

-

A couple at the heart of the community

The methodical beat of the car indicator signals a turning point in the Crabtree's lives, as they swing right off the busy A590 to take the winding path towards their future. They drive through familiar hinterlands and follow each turn in the rural road with care and precision. As they near the end, the tunnel of kaleidoscopic green hues gives way to more and more shades of grey as the couple edge closer to the village. Linda gives a knowing smile to David - they are where they are meant to be.

Together they sink into the soft red window seats in the Kings Arms with a glass of wine and a pint of local ale, and look out to the place they long to call home. Taking her last sips of wine, Linda places her glass down on the table and rises from her seat, ready to take action. 'Come on David, let's go and see if someone is in' she says. Their plan is already sketched out; the pair had spent the previous summer searching for houses for David's sister, who was now settled and very happy with her decision to purchase. After years of planning to move to the Lake District, they finally decided to turn their dreams into reality. Both are no strangers to the village, David has been coming here since he was a prep school child in Grange, when his parents brought him to Cartmel Races. These memories remained with him, and later as he and Linda were raising their two boys it became a family tradition to come to Cartmel for the races in May and August each year.

Linda leaves the pub striding purposefully, David attentively following behind. She knows the route, and marches over the bridge, to the side of the Priory and finally down a small road past the primary school. They look up at the stranger's house and with a brisk knock on the door wait

Linda and David Crabtree

to meet their fate. Through the translucent glass a short silhouette moves towards the door. As it opens, a soft, subdued voice says: 'Can I help you?' Linda explains that they had noticed the house was on the market a few months ago, and wanted to know if it will come back on.

The homeowner speaks gently and explains that her husband had died three days earlier, so it isn't such a good time, but nonetheless, etiquette prevails and she invites the pair in for a cup of tea. Exchanging numbers they reiterate their desire to buy the property and leave her with the option to sell to them. Two months later the deal is signed and the Crabtrees are about to embark on their final chapter.

The Crabtrees in Cartmel

The Crabtrees enjoy fine dining - regularly at Simon Rogan's restaurants - luxurious holidays, cups of tea, and of course days at the races. At home they sit by a log burning fire, surrounded by antique furniture decorated with family photos and white linen. Regulars in the local pubs, their sociable personalities mean that in one way or another they have befriended the whole village. Their son, Richard, lives over the hill, and his twins, their grandchildren, live in the village. So it is a place where they feel truly at home, and in Linda's words: 'We are happier here every day. There is always someone to talk to, and you know at our age it is nice to be part of a community. If one of us dies, we know that the other wouldn't be lonely and would be happy to live here.'

They will be the first to say that they have worked extremely hard for what they have. David took over the family business of running mills when his father retired, and Linda worked as an accountant for most of her life. After years of juggling jobs with raising their children, they were looking forward to retirement in Cartmel, vowing to lead a quiet life. But after three years, they were as active and engaged in the community as they had ever been. The two form a powerful duo, David with his planning skills and attention to detail and Linda with her ability to bring people together. These skills were soon noticed, and from doing the odd job for Cartmel in Bloom and other village events, the two suddenly found their roles had developed into something much more central. Now David chairs both Cumbria in Bloom and Cartmel in Bloom, and heads the Cartmel Village Society, and both are instrumental in making things happen in the village.

Cartmel in Bloom

Cartmel in Bloom is Cartmel's entry into the prestigious competition Britain in Bloom. A national horticultural campaign, it involves more than 1,100 cities, towns and villages that compete to be recognised for environmental responsibility, community participation and horticultural achievement. The competition is divided between regional and national competitions, and each year Cartmel in Bloom takes part in the Cumbrian regional competition.

Cumbria in Bloom came to Cartmel around 15 years ago, and was run by a local couple for many years. In 2011, the village suddenly had huge success in the Cumbria in Bloom competition and was then invited to participate in the Britain in Bloom competition. It was at this point that the small team realised they needed more help, and formed a committee and delegated key tasks across the village. Cartmel achieved reasonable success in the Britain in Bloom competition in 2012 and 2013, achieving a Silver Guild Award. Experience gained in the National Competition enabled Cartmel to gain the Gold Award in the Cumbria in Bloom Competition in 2014 and 2015.

It is a community effort now led by David. 'It is much more than planting bulbs and baskets', Linda emphasises, 'it is about pulling together the whole community to transform the village and give people a sense of pride and ownership of the place they live'. Cartmel in Bloom works with local businesses, schools and community members to implement an extensive year-round series of events, projects and activities. 'From Summer garden parties in the local pubs, wine tasting, ceilidhs, Christmas wreath making classes, bulb planting and maintenance around the village, there really is something for everyone to get involved with', Linda continues. They work with the local primary schools, and undertook a project where each child was involved with creating part of a large mosaic that is now displayed in the village bus stop.

It is an initiative that involves over 50 volunteers between the ages of 9 and 94. The monthly rota includes planting, watering, litter picking and pruning in key spots around the village, and their efforts do not go unnoticed. In June each year their work pays off and a colourful array of flowers subtly decorates every corner of the village. Although Linda and David make a huge effort to involve everyone in the village in Cartmel in Bloom, most of the people involved are over 50 years old. It requires dedicated effort and time to keep everything maintained, a luxury that young people with families just don't have. The changing demographics in the village also mean that there is a shortage of young people to get involved, and because of this the Crabtrees are concerned about the future of the organisation and the village more broadly.

Cartmel in flux

There is no denying that Cartmel has changed in recent years. The influx of tourism and newfound fame has had different effects on the village. Local businesses are flourishing as the constant flow of visitors means that they don't have to solely rely on local custom. However, for other locals, increased tourism and popularity has meant that house prices have significantly increased, and now many young people who were brought up in the village can no longer afford to live there. Homes that once housed local families are in some cases used as temporary holiday lets that wealthy owners retreat to once or twice a year.

Since arriving in the village, Linda and David have experienced this development first hand. As older generations die out on their street and their homes go on the market, the majority of houses are bought as second homes, or are rented out. Now their street is split in half between locals and holidaymakers. 'This is having a significant impact on the village and has changed the demographics. Fewer young people are able to afford housing in the village, which is affecting the local schools as there are less children to go', Linda explains. David chips in: 'Put it this way: there are five signs as you come into Cartmel from different directions, inside the parameters of those signs are about 270 properties, now probably around 50% of those are holiday homes, or to let. So there are only about 150 properties with people living in them, and most of these people are over 50'.

Looking to the future

The Crabtrees moved to the village in 2008, it was a seamless transition and they couldn't be happier with their decision. Alongside all the other community projects they take part in, they are working on a film project documenting the history of the village through oral histories and storytelling. Through this they hope to inform and inspire future generations to build on the past and continue to create a community they can be proud of. If you pay a visit in June, you will see their gardening efforts in full bloom, and you might even catch them around the village with a watering can, or perhaps they even have a spare spade so that you can lend them a hand.

Rachel Battersby

-

The devoted Headteacher

In the heart of Cartmel sits a small Victorian stonewalled building, with quaint blue doors, a long stained glass window covered in child-like designs, and a garden complete with a greenhouse and sunflower murals. Inside, the walls are adorned with colourful works created by young minds – pictures, stories and poems – each one uniquely expressing the new topics learnt. As the children arrive, they take off their coats, hanging them in the entrance on their individually named pegs. With only 74 children in total, in Cartmel C of E Primary School every child has a name and a face, and each one is warmly welcomed and greeted as they enter their classrooms. They take their seats and wait for the day's lessons to begin. Headteacher Mrs Battersby takes her stage at the front. Pen in hand, she begins, the first question of the day: What makes Cartmel C of E Primary School special to you?

The first child immediately raises her hand: 'People play with each other', and soon others follow:

'We are helpful and kind'.

'All the people in Cartmel Village are really kind'.

'The scenery!'

'Everyone is friendly in our village'.

Rachel Battersby

'A community'.

'I love that at school everyone trusts each other'.

'Everyone comforts one another if they are sad or lonely or just need someone to talk to'.

'It is a lovely place where people live right next door to each other and play together'.

'Cartmel Priory Church!'

This sense of pride is inbuilt from an early age, and after a short story, next on the morning's agenda is a trip to the Priory Church. Under instruction the pupils stand, tuck their chairs in and join hands in pairs as they are led round the corner to the Priory. Rev'd Nick Devenish is waiting patiently in the church porch, ready to inspire the next generation of potential worshippers. Inside, the children separate out into small teams as they learn about reflective Christian practices within the safety of the awe-inspiring Priory. This is one of the things that first attracted Rachel Battersby to Cartmel. As a practising Christian, a Church of England school was a perfect match for her, and she found her ideal job in a village steeped in such a rich religious history.

Coming to Cartmel

Rachel began her career in theatre, which seems apt for a primary school teacher, as each day requires an engaging performance of stamina and endurance. She was involved in a whole variety of shows, from performing Shakespeare classics in prestigious venues such as the Lowry, to musical productions, to delivering educational workshops in drama and singing. One of her most memorable jobs involved touring with the National Trust Theatre Company with an outdoor production. Collectively devised, the performance looked at environmental issues, such as land and conservation. They travelled all across the country performing in beautiful listed manor houses and vast gardens, warmly greeted everywhere with scones, tea and cakes.

Soon Rachel's career in theatre was in full swing. She had multiple performances lined up, and also founded her own theatre company, which was just taking off with a packed schedule across the North West of England. Then suddenly some life-changing news that would change her life path completely. Her husband was diagnosed with leukemia, and so all their priorities shifted as they focused on how to deal with his illness. It was no longer feasible for Rachel to travel the country, and she put everything on hold so that she could stay closer to home and look after him. It was during this time that she made the decision to follow in the footsteps of her mother and grandfather and retrain as a teacher. 'Teaching is in my blood', Rachel explains, 'it's something that I would have probably ended up going into eventually anyway, and I've never looked back'.

Born and raised in Accrington in Lancashire, Rachel is a true Northern lass. She is a home girl at heart, and has spent most of her life working in the North of England. Her first teaching job was at Dean Gibson Catholic Primary School in Kendal, where she worked herself up the ranks to become a SENCo (Special Educational Needs Co-ordinator) and Assistant Head. After six years she was looking for a change, but was not in any rush to move if she didn't find the right place.

'I always said that I would only apply for a headship if I got that certain feeling when I went to visit. I came to Cartmel having never set foot in the school before, and I knew straight away that this was the place for me. I went home and said "I'm going to go for it". It is a Church of England school, so as a practising Christian it fit in with my values. The big hall was also a huge selling point for me, as I wanted a space where the children could create drama and theatre. Oh, and I loved the stained-glass window created from the children's and parents' designs – seeing all this I just knew it had the type of community feel I was looking for'.

The school has met all her expectations. She loves working in a small school where there is time to nurture and get to know every child. The school is also very much rooted within the local community, and with so many things right on the doorstep it is easy to take the children into the local area.

Mighty Oaks from Little Acorns Grow

There has been a great deal of concern in the UK over the future of small schools: funding cuts, fewer resources and staff shortages all place increased demands on already stretched schools. As we talk, Rachel explains that these pressures also affect Cartmel. She uses the recent example of cuts to funding previously given to small schools, enabling them to provide free school meals to infants. Since this is a statutory obligation the school will have to find this money from elsewhere in their already limited budget. Another major concern is the changing demographics of the village, and the effect this might have on the future numbers at the school. Although Rachel recognises that tourism has helped the village to thrive, if more houses are bought up as second homes and holiday lets, fewer families can live in the village and therefore fewer children will come to the school. The consequences of these trends are only just beginning to show, but Rachel is hopeful that the new builds around the area will provide an opportunity for families to buy more affordable homes in the village. Despite these pressures, in Cartmel and the surrounding area there is a lot of local support, both from other schools who share resources, and in the wider community.

Cartmel C of E Primary School is very much embedded within the village. It is easy to engage with all aspects of village life, and the teachers take full advantage of this, creatively linking lesson plans with outings and activities. You can see evidence of this all around, inside the bus stop the back wall is covered in an elaborate blue mural, each piece designed and created by a pupil from the school.

Recently the school has been working with David and Linda Crabtree and Cartmel in Bloom, to encourage the children to take a pride in their environment through litter picking. They have worked with Simon Rogan and L'Enclume Farm, helping to plant, water and grow the organic vegetables used in his restaurant. Then, of course, they visit the Priory Church and form worship teams, and take part in Christian events throughout the year. These relationships create a sense of pride in the minds of the children, connecting them with the environment they live in, and teaching them the importance of being part of a wider community.

For now, the school is thriving, and has a strong community of people who are committed to giving the children who go there the best chance in life possible. 'It is a place where each child is valued as an individual, they are listened to, and this will help them to gain self belief and confidence needed for later life', Rachel states. Their mission statement - 'Mighty Oaks from Little Acorns Grow' - illustrates their belief that every child should be encouraged to realise their full potential, because great things can come from small beginnings.

Dr Paul Williams

-

Headteacher at Cartmel Priory School

'When I applied for the Headship at Cartmel Priory C of E School, the closest I had been to Cartmel was the Holker Garden Festival 20 years earlier. I didn't know the village at all - I hadn't even heard of Cartmel Sticky Toffee Pudding! I applied for the post primarily because the school sounded like a place where teachers could really get to know and help the students in their school community, plus I have always loved Cumbria. Having had leadership roles in various schools, from inner-city, multi-cultural schools to a high performing grammar school, nothing has given me more satisfaction than seeing Cartmel placed amongst the top performing schools in the country for progress pupils make. It has, therefore, been both a privilege and a pleasure. Cartmel really is special, from its links with the tumultuous events of the Angevin Empire to its delightful welcoming community and wonderful rural location. I am sure our pupils are aware of the unique secondary school opportunity offered here'.

Dr Paul Williams

George Broadhurst

-

The man who's seen it all

9am on a Monday morning in the late 1990s and the week, for George, begins like any other: breakfast and a coffee followed by carrying his wooden chair outside, and centring it directly in front of the Priory Hotel. He spends each day here – tea towel thrown over his shoulder, touting for business by shouting to passers-by and encouraging them to enter his establishment. The Priory Hotel is located in the middle of the Square and this chair places George at the heart of the village, and from here he sees it all. He knows the name of every person, visitor, dog walker, drinker and worker and as they pass by, each one receives a loud, light-hearted greeting. Today this includes a horse and rider who unsuspectingly trot past and George bellows to them in his deep Cumbrian accent, 'Nice arse on that, and the horse's isn't bad either', chuckling to himself.

Although a regular drinker inside the pubs during the evening, throughout the day George keeps his eyes on the two pubs in the Square from the outside. Over the years he has watched as the pubs have closed and reopened time and time again, as the landlords he befriended were drowned in drink and debt. He has seen generation after generation pass through the doors of the Royal Oak and the Kings Arms, each bringing their own troubles and merits and each one receiving a cheeky comment or two from the chair.

During his early years at the Priory Hotel every house in the Square belonged to a local family, including his own. George raised his children in the village and he knew all his neighbours, and could tell you the names and the business of every person in every house. But as the nineties became

George Broadhurst

the noughties, one by one the houses on the Square and around the village became either second homes, holiday cottages or shops, and for better or worse Cartmel was transforming into something different, and George had a front row seat.

Choose George's adventure

Although time passes chronologically, each life event influences another, and sometimes something that happened in the past can influence something far in the future. For this reason I'm going to tell you George's story in order, but I'm going to give you – the reader – the choice of how his life and adventures were formed. At the end of each section you will be given a choice of where in his life you want to go and use this to learn about how each event impacts the other.

So let us start at the beginning. Born in High Bankside Farm in 1938, George was raised as part of a farming community. But as World War II took hold and his father went into the army, they were given a Ministry of Defence house down in Flookburgh to live in during the war. At primary school George and his other classmates used to look out of the windows as the German and English Spitfires flew overhead, locked in battle as they defended the coastline and the shipyard in Barrow. Each day as the tide went out, the war became even more visible when big concrete blocks surfaced in the sand to prevent the Germans from landing there.

George remembers going to the station to see his father off and the platforms were full of military personnel, either guarding the station or boarding the train. As a child he didn't fully understand what was happening, but he saw all the wives and girlfriends weeping and waving their loved ones off, and children looking confused in amongst the chaos. 'It was awful, but everyone helped each other', he emphasises.

George is the eldest son of a dozen children, and spent a lot of his childhood working on the farm. He got his first job in the TD Smiths in Grange (now the Spar), where he got paid £1.19 and a penny a week. 'The first week I took the bus from Ravenstown to Grange and they charged me 46p for the ticket – almost half of my wages', George says, still shocked. So after the first week, in order to save money, he decided to start running to work, six miles there and six miles back. He only worked at TD Smiths for just over a year, and then started work on a farm again where he got paid four times as much - £4 and 1 shilling a week. 'There were two daily milk rounds, one in the morning and another early afternoon, and I would run four miles a day during the milk round, and then another couple to get back home', George concludes.

- To discover how this influenced his work ethic go to: George the grafter
- To discover how running to work influenced him go to: George the runner

George the runner

George returned to Cartmel in 1961 and found that years of running to and from work had made him extremely fit and extremely fast. His talents were noticed, and a local man began to train and enter George into races. He paid a shilling for him to take part in his first race, where he was greeted by a competitive top racer. 'Straightaway the racer asked me if I had ever run before, and I said no, so he gave me a 100 yard head start', George explains. 'It was a 220 yard track and I caught him up from behind and finished first. This made him very angry'.

He was a naturally gifted runner and trained for three years under a renowned coach named Denis Watts. Watts was one of the coaches who laid the foundations for Britain's impact on athletics over his 40-year career. He built up the sport in schools and clubs and trained some of the highest achieving athletes. He would bring the England and Lancashire teams for training in the fells behind Cartmel. 'He brought the reporters and cameraman from a magazine called *World Sports*. George recalls: 'It was the May 1962 edition, and there is a four page spread of me with the rest of the team. I remember on the cover was a footballer who at the time held the record payment for a transfer at that time, £65,000 [...] How times have changed.'

Although his sports career was short-lived George learnt many lessons. He discovered that the only way to win in life is by training hard: 'You have got to be able to recover fast from a knock, and push through your pain barrier, then you know you are winning'.

- To discover how this influenced George in business go to: George the businessman

George the grafter

Following his running career George decided to pursue another path. He used the knowledge he gained of building walls from working on farms, to work on the Backbarrow bypass, and also to change the wall on Windermere Lake so that the water from there could travel to Manchester to increase their water supplies.

In 1967 he travelled up North to work on building the M6 near Tebay. 'The other men were distracted by women and drink, but I was focused on the job', George remembers. He started buying wagons for £100 and contracted the other workers to run them, this was his first leap into the world of entrepreneurialism. From here he started in Heysham Power Station with a pick and shovel and in his own words 'worked like no other man'. His boss asked if he could get more men like him, so he found four more. The next week he wanted even more, so George got them and started to increase his earnings.

- To discover more about George's entrepreneurialism go to: George the businessman
- To discover how these experiences inspired George to get into racing go to: George the racer

George the singer

George was also a professional singer for many years, and went by the name of Mel Car (inspired by Cartmel). At one point he was almost offered a contract from the renowned Decca Records but they wanted a speciality act so it wasn't right for him. But if you're around in Cartmel on karaoke night you might hear George singing, in his soulful Frank Sinatra-esque way.

- To discover how these lungs helped him to win big go to: George the racer

George the businessman

George's running career gave him the determination to succeed, which, combined with his eye for opportunity, meant that he was extremely savvy in business. His main efforts and investments in business have been put into the Priory Hotel. He bought the hotel in 1994 as a derelict building and spent a lot of money restoring it.

'It has always been a hotel, and was the only hotel in the village for a long time', George explains as he comes back in with an old photograph of the Square taken in 1908, in which the Priory Hotel looks similar to today. 'There was an extension built onto Priory Hotel when the Duke of Devonshire's daughter married the Earl of Strathmore, so that they could house the extra guests. This was probably one of the biggest weddings ever held in Cartmel Priory', he says looking nostalgically into the picture.

Others may have come and gone but The Priory Hotel is one of the longest running businesses in the village. In 2010 they spent a lot of money renovating it into a luxury hotel: they enhanced the traditional features and modernised it, making it one of the best hotels in the village. A few years ago George passed the business on to his two sons Steven and Gary, and Gary's partner Julie, who are always there to greet you with a welcoming smile and a chat.

- **It is here that George spent many an hour sitting on his chair out the front, so to discover how George is a man of the community go to: From Cartmel, with love.**

George the racer

Following a tip-off from one of his work friends in Peterhead, George turned to horse racing to create extra income. He started in 1972 and has been in it ever since, he has owned sixteen horses during that time, and still owns some now that are cared for by his sister. In around 1978 he had the third best horse in the country – Pinkerton Man – that won its first two races. 'If we sold him then we would have made £250,000, but we kept it', he says, emphasising Pinkerton's worth. The horse was trained by Gordon Richard, and 'at first I was one of those owners who thought they knew more than the trainer', George admits. 'This led to mismanagement of the horse and entering him into races he wasn't ready for. But I learnt from this, and we had some good wins and good times'. George, of course, won many races in Cartmel racecourse with his horses, but the biggest was in 1979 with a horse called Bury Lord.

George also had a prize-winning dog called Rose and Crown, that took part in hound trailing races, one of Cumbria's oldest sports. Hound trailing involves the laying of a scent using a mixture of paraffin and aniseed oil, which is then followed by the hounds throughout the race. As the hounds near the finish, the owners stand at the finish line shouting and blowing whistles in an attempt to get their hound in first. I'm not surprised George had a few winners in this, as I have heard his loud voice echoing across the village for years.

Following his success on the tracks George set up a betting shop in 1973, then bought his second in 1974 and in the end he had acquired a collection of five betting shops across the area. These ran successfully for many years until he handed them over to pursue other things.

From Cartmel, with love

George raised his family in Bank House on the Square in Cartmel. In his own words, he has 'one daughter and quite a few sons', some of whom were raised in the village. 'I remember when Cartmel Primary School was on the verge of closing, as there were only seven children in the school during the early 1970s and four of them were mine', he says.

Cartmel has a special place in George's heart, and he knows its history and each and every change in the village like the back of his hand. As we talk he shares little snippets of his knowledge. For example, Cartmel was once known as Chertmel, named by the monks of the Priory, the name derived from 'Chert', rocky ground, and 'mel', a little stream, and then the locals changed it to Cartmel over time. Another interesting piece of history I learnt is that the bridge was built only 200 years ago. Before then people used to get across over the ford (shallow crossing) by the side of the Kings Arms – that's why it is called Ford Road today. He also explained that inside the building next to the Priory, where Cartmel Coffee is now located, there used to be the well of the village: 'It was ten foot deep and five foot wide, and the people who bought it in 1993 just filled it up with concrete. The village is an area of conservation, but what have they conserved if this was allowed to be destroyed?' he questions passionately.

'Now in Cartmel, there is no village left, it's all holiday cottages. Don't get me wrong, I don't mind visitors, visitors are a good thing, they bring lots of money, but it is a shame that young people are unable to move back to the village', George laments. As we have seen, George has made a good life for himself in Cartmel, seizing opportunities and leading a life that turned in many directions and that was filled with adventure. In his own words 'I love women, love my work, love sport, and most I love my village and my family', and it all came from Cartmel, with love.